THE SECURE FREEDOM STRATEGY

A Plan for Victory Over the Global Jihad Movement

By the Tiger Team

CENTER FOR SECURITY POLICY PRESS

The Secure Freedom Strategy:
A Plan for Victory Over the Jihadist Movement is published
in the United States by the Center for Security Policy Press,
a division of the Center for Security Policy.

Published on January 28, 2015

Originally published as a white paper on January 16, 2015

THE CENTER FOR SECURITY POLICY
1901 Pennsylvania Avenue, Suite 201 Washington, DC 20006
Phone: (202) 835-9077 | Email: info@securefreedom.org
For more information, please see securefreedom.org

Book design by Adam Savit
Cover design by Alex VanNess

CONTENTS

TIGER TEAM CO-AUTHORS

- Lieutenant General William G. "Jerry" Boykin, US Army (Ret.)
- Ambassador Henry F. Cooper
- Fred Fleitz
- Kevin Freeman
- Frank J. Gaffney, Jr.
- Dan Goure
- John Guandolo
- Jim Hanson
- Brian Kennedy
- Clare M. Lopez
- Adm. James A. "Ace" Lyons, US Navy (Ret.)
- Joseph E. Schmitz
- Tom Trento
- J. Michael Waller
- Tommy Waller
- David Yerushalmi, Esq.

EXECUTIVE SUMMARY

For at least thirty-five years, the United States has been at war with enemies sworn to its destruction. It did not seek enmity or hostilities with them. Both are the product of forces that long predated the establishment of this country, to say nothing of its adoption toward the end of the 20th Century of policies towards the Middle East or other regions.

For much of this period, the U.S. government has pursued various strategies – including selective military engagements, benign neglect, willful blindness and outright appeasement – that have in common one very low common denominator: They all ignore the aforementioned realities and, as a practical matter, have exacerbated them.

A lack of clarity about these realities or a strategy for dealing effectively with them has contributed to a strategic environment of great and growing danger and a wholly inadequate American capacity for contending with such perils. This paper recommends corrective actions, starting with a clear-eyed understanding of the enemy we confront – namely, an international, ideologically driven Global Jihad Movement and its enablers – and the essential elements of an effective strategy for countering it. The alternative approach is modeled after the successful strategy President Ronald Reagan pursued to defeat Soviet communism, embodied in his National Security Decision Directive (NSDD) 75.

UNDERSTANDING THE ENEMY'S THREAT DOCTRINE

First and foremost, the United States needs to achieve a clear understanding of the enemy and its doctrine. That requires, in particular, clarity concerning the ideology its adherents call shariah, the jihad it impels and the various ways in which such warfare is being waged against us.

The term "shariah" as used in this paper is intended to denote the authoritative and authoritarian *corpus juris* of Islamic law as it has been articulated by the recognized shariah authorities since at least the 10th century. This use of the term shariah, therefore, does not refer to an idiosyncratic, personal or purely pietistic observance of Islamic law which may or may not conform to the entirety of established Islamic doctrine. As used in this document, the descriptor "shariah-adherent" does not apply to the latter, but rather to Islamic supremacists who engage in jihad or support those who do in furtherance of the political goals of their ideology.

This jihadist doctrine is being advanced by both violent techniques and by means other than terrorism, the latter often pursued technically within the law to avoid detection and countermeasures. Practitioners of such stealthy forms of jihad depend on the U.S. propensity to focus exclusively on "countering violent extremism," while they pursue their end goals through subversive methods that do not presently use violence. We must, accordingly, be prepared to deal kinetically where necessary with the perpetrators of violent jihad and no less effectively through other means with what the Muslim Brotherhood calls "civilization jihad" – its seditious, covert program designed to "destroy Western civilization from within…by [our own] hands."[1]

Ironically, it has been incidents of violent jihad – including the Fort Hood massacre[2], the Boston Marathon bombing[3], the beheading of a grandmother in Oklahoma[4] and the imposition of shariah blasphemy laws via murders in France – that have brought the elements of *pre*-violent jihad into sharp relief. This includes a successful "information dominance" campaign and other influence operations that keep us from understanding:

- who was responsible for such attacks (i.e., Muslims whose self-described "religious fervor" prompted them to wage jihad against the United States and the West);

- the infrastructure being built to support jihad inside the United States (e.g., the shariah-adherent mosques, Islamic Centers, and other indoctrination and ideological warfare centers attended by each of the perpetrators that have been tied to an organization that federal prosecutors have identified as part of "the Muslim Brotherhood's infrastructure in America," namely, the North American Islamic Trust [NAIT][5]);

- the double-standard applied to Muslim perpetrators of violence contrasted with the treatment of those of other faiths; and

- the perils of submitting to demands for restrictions on freedom of expression or other liberties.

ESTABLISHING OUR OBJECTIVE

It is the sworn duty of every U.S. official to uphold and defend "the Constitution of the United States against all enemies, foreign and domestic." A strategic objective of the Global Jihad Movement is to subvert or overthrow the Constitution of the United States. Therefore, our fundamental objective in opposing the Global Jihad Movement, and its attempts to promote its ideology in the United States, is to defend our Constitution and the freedoms it guarantees here at home.

Cold War-era resistance to Communism was not merely against the Soviet government, but against Communist ideological offensives to subvert or overthrow our Constitution. To face the Global Jihad threat, the United States must enunciate a national commitment to – using a phrase President Reagan employed as the object of NSDD 75 – "contain and over time reverse" shariah-driven Islamic expansionism, including establishment of a Caliphate. The rising tide of shariah supremacism and its manifestations here and abroad make abundantly clear that Western civilization, indeed America, cannot coexist with the Global Jihad Movement. Nor can we fight or win this struggle alone: American allies worldwide face the same threat from the same Global Jihad Movement. Forging strong partnerships with our closest friends in Australia, Canada, Europe, Israel, New Zealand, and elsewhere and standing with them — and, indeed, all who choose liberty — is the surest way to demonstrate the unified resolve of the civilized world to confront savagery and spare it the blight of shariah.

At a minimum, we must practice the most basic principle of a foreign policy rooted in the philosophy of peace through strength: It should be far better to be an ally of the United States than its enemy. Only by conducting our affairs in this fashion do we have stand a chance of decisively thwarting the efforts of aggressive jihadists, and their enablers, to increase the number and lethality of our foes and neutralize or eliminate our friends.

For starters, we should not be encouraging the jihadis to undertake a redoubled effort to make us, in the words of the Quran, "feel subdued" through intensifying violence. Yet, that is precisely what the doctrine of shariah commands its adherents to do in the face of acts of submission by infidels. As long as we seek – in the name of "political correctness," "multiculturalism," "diversity," or "tolerance" – to accommodate or appease shariah's adherents, they are *obliged* to respond with increasing acts of violent jihad.

In short, the Global Jihad Movement must be thwarted in its efforts to impose shariah upon us, whether through violent jihad techniques or through pre-violent jihad (using Dawah tactics) promoted by the Muslim Brotherhood until the correlation of forces is ripe for the decisive use of force.

REESTABLISHING 'PEACE THROUGH STRENGTH'

Just as President Reagan did in his day, the contemporary hollowing out of the U.S. military must be reversed as a matter of the utmost priority. The perception of American weakness only reinforces and encourages our shariah-adherent enemies' conviction that the time has come for intensifying jihad operations. That perception is also emboldening other adversaries, including Russia, China and North Korea, while in turn weakening our allies and friends, and undermining national morale here at home.

As a result, restoring and enhancing the power-projection capabilities of our armed forces is not only necessary to ensure we have the range of capabilities necessary to address those threats kinetically. It is also vital if we are to minimize the chances we will needlessly have to fight wars that might otherwise be deterred and, hence, avoided.

As the United States is not confronting just terrorist organizations, or even their state-sponsors, but prospectively "peer competitors," the rebuilding of American military power must be balanced across the spectrum of nuclear, missile defense, conventional and special operations forces. We must also continue to develop asymmetric capabilities (e.g., in space and cyber space) while correcting our most egregious vulnerabilities to these enemies' asymmetric attacks (notably, electromagnetic pulse, cyberwarfare, counter-space, economic/financial warfare, smuggled weapons of mass destruction, etc.)

COUNTER-IDEOLOGICAL WARFARE

As in the Cold War, America's ability to challenge and neutralize its enemies' animating ideology is at least as important as the task of countering their kinetic threats. Once we are clear about the nature and centrality of the shariah doctrine to the existential danger we currently face, the need for a serious and effective counter-ideological strategy becomes self-evident.

In fact, some American military leaders are now beginning to recognize that they are aware of their lack of understanding of the ideological threat. "We do not understand the movement, and until we do, we are not going to defeat it," a senior general officer recently admitted in the context of countering the Islamic State. "We have not defeated the idea. We do not even understand the idea."[6]

President Reagan understood that at the core of his NSDD 75 strategy had to be a robust assertion of the superiority of our constitutional republic and civilization – and a concomitant effort to delegitimate and undermine our enemies' totalitarian form of government and repressive ideology. A similar foundation is essential for countering today's foes, jihadis and others who seek to crush human liberty.

In particular, such a strategy requires that we direct our support, legitimating and outreach efforts to *non-Jihad* Muslims, and deny it to the jihadis (most especially, the Muslim Brotherhood). This is critical to empowering the former and de-legitimating the latter. It is also essential if we are to thwart the shariah-adherents' concerted bid to dominate the non-adherent Muslim community and compel it to conform to shariah.[7]

The strategy can be done within a framework of religious tolerance by focusing on shariah's supremacist and jihad elements as the enemy's threat doctrine, thereby avoiding a frontal assault on the Muslim faith. To be clear, shariah's adherents insist that they are one and the same and that any Muslim who believes otherwise is an apostate, which is a capital offense. Yet, surely there exists some unknowable number of Muslims around the world – and especially in this country – who, in disobedience to the authorities of their faith, do not themselves subscribe to the jihad elements of shariah, and do not seek to impose it on others. Indeed, many who came to this country did so at least in part to escape shariah.[8]

The point that the *authorities* of Islam are part of the problem – not "violent extremists" who are said to be trying to "hijack Islam" was made plain when Egyptian president Abdel Fatah al-Sisi challenged the leadership of Al-Azhar University in Cairo, (often described as the Vatican of Islam). [9]

Unfortunately, no significant elements from within Islam thus far have presented themselves as likely allies in the death struggle we confront with our mutual enemies. So it is important that, even as we continue to encourage and support any who do, we not distract ourselves from a focus on the majority of Muslims and Islamic authorities who continue to promote or at least support jihad and shariah supremacism unabated.

Putting a counter-strategy into practice will require, first and foremost, identifying the Muslim Brotherhood for the explicitly jihadist organization it has always been and is now. Continuing to treat its operatives and organizations (overt and covert) in America and overseas as "partners" because we are told they "eschew violence" is a formula for our incremental destruction.

The Brotherhood, its funders, ideologues (notably, Yousef al-Qaradawi) and propagandists (especially Al-Jazeera) should be regarded as enemies of the United States. At best, they are engaged in material support for terrorism. At worst, they are perpetrators, as well as enablers, of it. Wherever they are to be found, and as soon as possible, these foes should be neutralized as political forces. At a minimum, they must be denied access to U.S. government agencies, arms, funds, and, via television cable packages, household subscribers. New legislation would be required first to designate the Muslim Brotherhood an Enemy of the State, a Hostile Foreign Power, or Terrorist Organization to enable legally such bans against it.

Others enabling the Muslim Brotherhood and its fellow jihadis (which include al-Qaeda and other practitioners of the explicitly violent jihad) must be regarded as part of the problem, not as reliable allies. Thus, we must confront with intent to defeat not only the jihad regime in Iran. We cannot continue to give a pass to Saudi-, Qatari- and other Gulf State 'frenemies' that are – despite their theological differences with the Iranian Shiites – perfectly prepared to make common cause with them against Western "infidels" as the Saudis did in the 9/11 attacks.

These Sunni governments support the Global Jihad Movement through asymmetric warfare techniques (notably: underwriting information and influence operations; the construction and management of shariah-adherent mosques, Islamic Centers, and indoctrination and training centers; the migration of shariah-adherent populations to non-Muslim countries; and underwriting jihad cells and organizations) at the very same time they are, to varying degrees, allied with us to protect their ruling families and interests by hosting our forces in their countries.

The United States also needs to check and defeat what is arguably the single most important instrument of political warfare now being wielded *against us* by our shariah-adherent enemies: the Organization of Islamic Cooperation (OIC). The OIC has to be opposed, not abetted, in its efforts – both through multilateral forums (in particular, UN agencies) and bilaterally – to impose shariah blasphemy laws and other, incremental measures in the service of advancing its ideology at the expense of our constitutional rights and freedom more generally.

Every instrument of the U.S. government – especially a reconstituted and state-of-the-art information warfare capability comparable to that brought to bear at the height of the Cold War by Radio Free Europe/Radio Liberty and the U.S. Information Agency, and utilizing social media and other technologies not available in that era – must be employed to wrest information dominance from our enemy. Critical to this effort is the recruitment and training of professional cadres willing and able to execute the strategy.

INTELLIGENCE OPERATIONS

We must take a page from the playbook developed during the Reagan administration by then-Director of Central Intelligence William Casey and use covert means as permitted in federal statutes and EO 12333 wherever possible to counter, divide, and undermine our enemies. To the traditional intelligence techniques should be added aggressive use of psychological operations, cyberwarfare and, where necessary, clandestine and special operations. These efforts require an overhaul of legal authority to make them effective.

A particular focus must be challenging the inroads being made by jihadis using funding, arms, and shariah indoctrination to dominate Muslim populations and enlist them in jihad. This will require making shariah-adherence a differentiator between those we will support and those we must oppose. Such a differentiation also will clarify the true status of so-called 'lone wolves,' whose self-adherence to shariah makes it more accurate to describe them as jihadis acting individually to further a shared goal: the global triumph of their ideology.

ECONOMIC WARFIGHTING

As with the Reagan NSDD 75 plan, there must be a central economic/financial warfighting component to a new American strategy for defeating the existential enemies of our time. This component would include:

- Constricting the principal source of revenues for the jihad: vast petrodollar transfers from Western nations to OPEC states that are the wellsprings of support for Islamic expansionism and the Organization of Islamic Cooperation. Burgeoning energy supplies within this country and in our neighbors to the north and south offer opportunities for leverage that can be used to defund OPEC and bankrupt both those dependent on its underwriting of jihad and those who sponsor such warfare.

  For example, we can exploit natural gas and natural gas-derived methanol as transportation fuels, allowing the sector that is the principal U.S. consumer of foreign oil, and the nation as a whole, to be weaned from what remains currently of their dependency on supplies from outside the hemisphere (currently some three million barrels per day).

  An additional benefit from ensuring that most cars operating today can utilize alcohol-based fuels as well as gasoline would be to enable more than 100 countries around the world to produce such fuels from their own feedstocks (namely, such carbon-rich resources as natural gas, coal, switch grass, trash, wood chips, biomass, etc.) The potential for electric cars may also be part of this mix. The practical effect of such energy independence – not just in this country, but world-wide – would be to break the back of the OPEC cartel.

- Treating shariah-adherents in the global financial markets and international trading system the same way as terrorists – namely, by stigmatizing them. This would mean, among other things, reversing the present practice of accommodating and even *encouraging* shariah finance – a technique employed by civilization jihadis to penetrate and subvert our capitalist system.[10]

- Exposing shariah-inspired sovereign wealth funds as instruments of financial jihad. Ending the practice of providing undisciplined, discretionary cash to shariah-linked entities (e.g., sovereign sponsors, wealth funds, banks, companies, bond and equity offerings, etc.) that currently can attract large-scale financing without any underlying projects or trade transactions. For example, shariah-associated entities have benefited enormously from so-called "structured commodity finance" transactions (a.k.a. "pre-export finance") of the kind that has been used to make available multi-billion-dollar, front-end cash infusions to bad actors in exchange for future deliveries of oil and other commodities at a discounted price.

- Requiring that all U.S. equity funds, banks, brokerage houses, and the like disclose the degree of investment in, or investment by, sharia-compliant entities would contribute in a significant way to transparency in such matters.

CYBER WARFARE

As noted above, one of the increasingly ominous aspects of warfare in the 21st Century is the opportunity for asymmetric attacks across various domains and technologies. Among the most rapidly intensifying and proliferating of these is cyber warfare.

The shariah-inspired enemy is operating in loose collaboration with an array of adversarial nation states, sub-national terrorist organizations and transnational anarchists, cyber warriors and hackers. Clearly, not all of these collaborators share a commitment to Islamic supremacism. But all of them appear, broadly-speaking, to agree with any agenda aimed at destroying Western civilization – or at a minimum, are willing to work for wealthy clients.

Highly sophisticated and potentially destructive cyber espionage and warfare tools increasingly in the hands of this nation's enemies are capable of targeting: classified government operations, the databases of international firms, individuals' private information, social media forums, and perhaps most alarmingly of all, the critical infrastructure of societies across the globe. The very connectivity that is the hallmark of advanced economies everywhere has become their most exposed vulnerability.

Additionally, the cyber battlespace intersects with each of the others we address in this paper: the kinetic-military, ideological, intelligence, and economic arenas. Operating behind the scenes, the Global Jihad Movement's so-called "cyber armies" and their associates move adroitly across the Internet to communicate, proselytize, recruit, train and launch attacks that threaten not just our credit card data and social security numbers, but the very systems that make modern life possible. With the known ability to breach the firewalls that are supposed to protect the U.S. electric grid, energy distribution, water supply networks and other indispensable infrastructures, jihadist nation states like Iran, as well as malicious associations like "Anonymous" today constitute the kind of threat to our national existence that previously was posed exclusively by a massive nuclear attack.

Therefore, a new strategy that addresses these threats must also be able to draw upon capabilities largely unknown at the time of President Reagan's NSDD 75: The ability to counter cyber threats and to employ our own cyber operations against America's adversaries. To do so will entail a whole-of-government – and indeed, whole-of-society – response, enlisting the best and brightest of our technical minds for decades to come.

CIVILIZATION JIHAD ON THE HOMEFRONT

Just as the United States must understand and decisively counter the violent jihadis, it must do the same with respect to those engaged in *pre*-violent forms of subversive warfare that the Muslim Brotherhood calls civilization jihad.

The Brotherhood has had considerable success with the latter since the Muslim Students Association, its first front organization in America, was established in 1962. Among its accomplishments have been: keeping the "infidels" ignorant of the true nature and progress of efforts to insinuate shariah into Western societies; demanding and securing accommodations for shariah-adherent Muslims and other concessions; utilizing and exploiting educational vehicles to promote the cause of Islamic supremacism; "bridge-building" and interfaith "dialogue" to suborn clerics of other faiths and enlist them as protectors of subversive shariah on First Amendment grounds; promoting Shariah-Compliant Finance; insinuating shariah into U.S. courts; and placing Muslim Brothers into positions from which they can exercise influence.

The following are illustrative examples of initiatives that would advance those goals necessary to rolling back the Muslim Brotherhood in America:

- Muslims who reject shariah's seditious agenda and oppose its imposition on others should be promoted and empowered. As part of this effort, federal and state-level government agencies must end the practice of "engagement" with or "outreach" to those who purport to be "leaders" of the Muslim American community but who often are, in fact, simply shariah- adherent Islamic supremacists associated with the Muslim Brotherhood.

- Congressional hearings should be held to explore crucial questions first raised about the extent of Brotherhood influence on U.S. policymaking in April 2012 by five U.S. lawmakers.[11] They sought Inspector General investigations of individuals who were either employees of or advisors to five federal agencies shown to have ties to or sympathies with the Muslim Brotherhood. The object was to establish whether such individuals were having an influence on U.S. policies that were increasingly aligning with the dictates of the Brotherhood.

- Legislation designating the Muslim Brotherhood as a terrorist organization should be adopted as a basis for rolling up and shutting down its front groups in the United States and ending any and all U.S. aid and military sales to any Muslim Brotherhood entities, including associates, front group or even "elected governments."

- Alternatively, new legislation that creates a listed category for "Hostile Foreign Powers" should be enacted to identify groups such as the Muslim Brotherhood whose threat is, for the moment at least, subversive rather than violent.

- Over eighty percent of U.S. mosques have been shown to be shariah-adherent and promoting jihad as evidenced in such visible characteristics as dress, beards, and male-female segregation; the content of preaching and sermons; and printed materials on display or for sale. They are incubators of, at best, subversion and, at worst, violence and should be treated accordingly.[12]

- The United States must terminate the practice of issuing visas for shariah-adherent imams who often seek to use such mosques for purposes antithetical to tolerant religious practice and to the Constitution.

- Similarly, the federal government must stop using refugee resettlement programs, political asylum, visa lotteries, amnesties, etc. to bring large numbers of shariah-adherent Muslims to this country.

- The U.S. must enforce existing immigration law that requires all immigrants to defend the U.S. Constitution "against all enemies, foreign and domestic," under the terms of their Naturalization Oath of Allegiance to the United States of America,[13] and to use shariah-adherent advocacy and practices as legal premises for deportation and stripping of American citizenship.

- American academic institutions that accept funds from shariah-adherent individuals or governments must be required to disclose fully the extent of such payments and the purpose for which they are provided. Where that purpose amounts to promoting shariah or civilization jihadist agendas (e.g., interfaith dialogue, "Muslim-Christian understanding," etc.), the institution should be discouraged from hosting such activities.

- Charitable organizations that operate as taxpayer-subsidized entities through tax-deductible contributions and promote shariah-adherent individuals and programs, should have their IRS 501(c)(3) status revoked.

- Academic institutions that receive federal funding and promote shariah-adherent individuals programs should be barred from receiving federal funds, including grants, contracts, scholarships, fellowships, subsidies, and proceeds from federally administered or subsidized student loans.

- Firms engaging in Shariah-Compliant Finance must be required to disclose the hostile nature of shariah, the names and roles of shariah advisors involved in investment decisions and the expectation that some of the proceeds may be used to support jihad by way of the *zakat* obligation.

In sum, the American people must be mobilized to comprehend the perilous state we are in and the necessity for concerted action to correct it. The first step is to adopt and begin to implement the concerted program described above, thus identifying for the public: the enemy we confront; how they are inspired, enabled, and sustained through various ideological, political, economic, financial, military, and paramilitary means; and the comprehensive steps necessary to defeat them.

With this foundation, it should be possible to effect the necessary second step: the adoption by the nation of a true warfooting that will bring to bear the popular vigilance and support that will make it possible for the rest of a NSDD 75 2.0 strategy to be fully executed.

INTRODUCTION

America is at war. It is not one of our choosing. Rather, this war has been waged against us since at least 1979, when the Islamic Republic of Iran began attacking U.S. assets, facilities, and nationals.

Since then, under successive presidential administrations and Congresses of both parties, we have engaged, to varying degrees, in hostilities with those who have declared war upon the United States and the West. Those efforts on our part have been mounted without clarity about the nature of our foes or what animates them, without enlisting the necessary support of the American people and without the full mobilization of U.S. assets to defeat the enemy.

In particular, the U.S. government has failed to recognize the role played in this war by an Islamic supremacist ideology its adherents call shariah. The term "shariah" as used in this paper is intended to denote the authoritative and authoritarian *corpus juris* of Islamic law as it has been articulated by the recognized shariah authorities since at least the 10th century. This use of the term shariah, therefore, does not refer to an idiosyncratic, personal, or purely pietistic observance of Islamic law which may or may not conform to the entirety of established Islamic doctrine. As used in this document, the descriptor "shariah-adherent" does not apply to the latter, but rather to Islamic supremacists who engage in jihad or support those who do in furtherance of the political goals of their ideology.

While a small part of this doctrine (by some estimates, ten percent) defines pietistic practices observed by Muslims the world over, the preponderance of the shariah code prescribes a comprehensive program for governing all aspects of life and for imposing it on others.

The latter elements specifically call for the practice of jihad – warfare (or struggle) using whatever means are available and necessary to achieve shariah's triumph. The faithful are obliged by shariah to engage in or otherwise to support jihad by means violent, non-violent, or pre-violent.

Not all Muslims espouse the entirety of shariah; nor do all embrace or conform to these requirements of shariah. But the authorities of Islam do and they consider those who do not to be apostates – a crime punishable by death under Islamic Law and in countries whose legal code is fully shariah-compliant.

As a result, the United States today faces a metastasizing and ever more perilous strategic environment. The Shiite Islamic regime in Iran that initiated this phase of what might be described as the long-running War for the Free

World, has persisted in its calls for the destruction of the West and its efforts to achieve that result. Indeed, the mullahs in Tehran are now on the cusp of realizing their decades-long ambition to acquire the nuclear weapons suitable for effecting what former Iranian president Mahmoud Ahmadinejad called "a world without America."[14]

Over the intervening years, Sunni jihadis inspired by the same political-military-legal shariah doctrine espoused by the Shiite mullahs of Iran[15], have mounted with increasing success their own efforts to impose worldwide shariah. Whether these jihadis identify themselves by such names as al-Qaeda, the Taliban, the Islamic State, Boko Haram, the al-Nusra Front, Hamas or the Muslim Brotherhood (whose organization and agenda spawned or inspired all the others), their goals are the same: force the entire world to submit to shariah and establish a political system to govern according to it under a ruler known as the Caliph.

The achievements to date of these and other elements of what is best described as the Global Jihad Movement (GJM) have, to varying degrees, benefited from and bolstered other state and non-state actors hostile to the United States. They have also provided these actors with new opportunities to expand their own abilities to challenge, subvert and, if they choose, to wage war against the United States and the West. As a result, we now confront a Russia, China, and even North Korea that are more formidable and emboldened adversaries. Any strategy for dealing with the global jihad must also address this reality.

In 2010, an informal group of nineteen civilian and military national security practitioners, analysts, and other experts known as Team B II joined forces to provide a "second opinion" on the nature and implications of the enemy threat doctrine. Their collective labors produced an important book entitled *Shariah: The Threat to America*. It strongly dissented from the official line ("Team A") to the effect that we are confronting isolated "terrorist" or "violent extremist" individuals or groups, who either have no particular animating creed (i.e., they are "self-radicalized" or "lone wolves") or they embrace an inaccurate and hateful version of Islam (i.e., they are "hijacking" a "religion of peace").

In late 2014, members of the original team have joined forces once again, augmented by others with valuable skill sets, at a time when the United States government is trying to develop and implement a "strategy" for countering a jihadist group calling itself the Islamic State.

The purpose of the Secure Freedom Strategy is to challenge the notion that any approach that takes aim primarily, let alone exclusively, at any one franchise of the Global Jihad Movement is doomed to fail. Instead, we advocate a comprehensive approach to address the reality that the United States and the West must confront that movement *as a whole* by, among other things, working to counter the dangerous, supremacist ideology of shariah that impels it.

To reiterate: Not all Muslims espouse the entirety of this doctrine of shariah. However, the shariah ideology absolutely *is* endorsed and practiced by the authorities of the faith, its most revered institutions, the 57 members of the Organization of Islamic Cooperation (the OIC, which includes Iran and the four Arab nations it now dominates – Iraq, Lebanon, Syria and Yemen) and the supranational Muslim Brotherhood.[16]

The Secure Freedom Strategy is intended to inform the unfolding debate on Capitol Hill and across America concerning revisions to the existing legal bases for countering al Qaeda and its associates, including franchises in North Africa, Nigeria, Yemen, and Somalia and its dangerous spin-off group operating in Iraq and Syria, the Islamic State. This alternative strategy could take the form of a new Authorization for the Use of Military Force (AUMF) or possibly a Declaration of War. Additionally, enforcement of existing U.S. laws with regard to sedition and treason, and application of principles already part of the Oath of Naturalization, for example, would go a long way toward mitigating the GJM threat in the domestic arena.

The deliberations expected to take place early in the 114th Congress over how to adapt U.S. policy to address new threats from assorted al Qaeda and similar groups offer a long-overdue opportunity to revisit the assumptions that have governed U.S. policy on the Global Jihad Movement at least since 9/11, and arguably since 1979.

Specifically, the United States can no longer: indulge in the illusion that "terrorism" or "violent extremism" is unrelated to the politico-military-legal requirements of shariah; rely upon adherents to shariah (notably, the Muslim Brotherhood, its front groups and operatives) as arbiters of what we can know, think, and do about this doctrine and the threat it poses; or deal strictly symptomatically with the violent elements of that threat while largely ignoring *pre*-violent elements such as those represented by the Brotherhood's "civilization jihad".

A new strategy is required if we are to survive, let alone prevail over, enemies that include not only al Qaeda, the Islamic State and the Muslim Brotherhood but other franchises and elements of the global jihad. The Tiger Team believes that a starting point for such a strategy is to adapt the comprehensive, systematic approach President Reagan devised and successfully implemented to defeat another totalitarian ideology devoted to world domination: Soviet Communism.

The Reagan strategy is described below. It was officially spelled out in the now-declassified National Security Decision Directive (NSDD) 75.[17] While there are notable differences between the two ideologies (e.g., communism is an expressly atheistic program, while shariah has a patina of religiosity that superficially obscures the true totalitarian nature of this ideology that has properly been described as "communism with a god."), the central elements of NSDD 75 are highly applicable to the effort to counter today's enemy threat doctrine of shariah.

This is a moment for a realism and clarity in American security policy. The U.S. has tried the alternative with respect to the Global Jihad Movement for the past thirty-five years with dismal results. Our men and women in uniform, their families, our nation's law enforcement, and – increasingly – its average citizenry, continue to pay the price for America's failure to properly engage this hostile ideology as it grows stronger with every act of weakness on the part of our nation's leadership. We must at this juncture employ, instead, a time-tested – and successful – approach to counter-ideological warfare. The Tiger Team is pleased to offer this plan for doing just that.

THE TEMPLATE: PRESIDENT REAGAN'S NATIONAL SECURITY DECISION DIRECTIVE 75

Ronald Reagan campaigned for the presidency in 1980 on a platform that rejected the policies of accommodation and détente towards the Soviet Union that had been pursued by administrations of both parties. When asked what his strategy toward the Kremlin would be, he famously responded, "We win. They lose."[18]

Mr. Reagan's views on the USSR and the threat it posed were strongly influenced by a classified study called "An Exercise in Competitive Analysis" commissioned by then-CIA Director George H.W. Bush and performed in 1976 by a group of independent national security experts that came to be known as "Team B." Team B found that the official National Intelligence Estimates concerning Soviet military capabilities and intentions (produced by the U.S. Intelligence Community or "Team A") seriously understated the threat.

The Soviets also presented a subversive political threat, undermining governments and societies worldwide, with a global "active measures" network to accomplish Moscow's military objectives through means that would not provoke an American military response. Team B was chaired by Dr. Richard Pipes, at the time a professor of history and specialist on Russia at Harvard University.[19]

After winning a sweeping electoral mandate in 1980 for, among other things, a new foreign policy direction, President Reagan issued a series of National Security Study Directives (NSSDs) to guide the formulation of new approaches. Two NSSDs issued in 1982 addressed U.S.-Soviet relations.[20] The principal author of the response to these directives was none other than Dr. Richard Pipes who had been recruited to serve as the Director of the Soviet Affairs at the National Security Council (NSC).[21]

What Pipes crafted was a study that was consistent with the instincts and attitudes of President Reagan regarding U.S. policy toward the Soviet Union: There was a need for radical change.

Pipes clearly laid out new goals for American policy. If the guiding American strategy of containment and détente placed a premium on maintaining the status quo, Pipes called for nothing less than the transformation of the Soviet Union. He argued that the Reagan administration's priorities should be: "1) The decentralization and demilitarization of the Soviet economy; 2) the weakening of power and privileged position of the ruling communist elite; and 3) gradual democratization of the USSR."

In short, the object would be to end the threat posed to America by Soviet communism and the state that sought to impose it worldwide, including on us.

Making that happen meant not engaging in concessions and naïve negotiations that had the effect, in seeking to appease the Soviet leadership, of perpetuating its misrule and inviting its further aggression. Instead, Pipes argued for an approach that was designed to undermine Soviet power. As Pipes put it, those goals could be accomplished by "exploit[ing] the vulnerabilities in Moscow's global situation."

In particular, the Soviet economy was struggling and the Kremlin leadership was despised by many. Pipes wanted to "exacerbate weaknesses in Soviet foreign and domestic policy," not make things easier for the leadership as American policy had done during the détente era. The idea was to do so without provoking a Soviet military response.

To that end, Dr. Pipes recommended that the U.S. take the ideological offensive. If moral equivalence had become all too common as America's posture on the global stage during previous presidencies, Pipes called for the U.S. to staunchly support and promote American ideals: "U.S. policy toward the Soviet Union must have an ideological thrust which clearly demonstrates the superiority of U.S. and Western values of individual dignity and freedom, a free press, free trade unions, free enterprise, and political democracy over the repressive character of Soviet communism."

This was more than talk. It was a prescription for action. The Pipes study also declared that the Reagan administration should "encourage democratic movements and forces to bring about political change inside these countries. In this connection, the U.S. must develop the means to extend U.S. support to individuals and movements that share the U.S. commitment to political democracy and individual freedom."

The Pipes plan was a call for a sea change in American strategic policy and practice toward the Soviet Union. "By identifying the promotion of evolutionary change within the Soviet Union itself as an objective of U.S policy, the United States takes the long-term strategic offensive. This approach therefore contrasts with the essentially reactive and defensive strategy of containment, which concedes the initiative to the Soviet Union and its allies and surrogates."

The "Response to NSSD 11-82," dated December 6, 1982, in turn, formed the foundation for National Security Decision Directive (NSDD) 75, signed by President Reagan on January 17, 1983. This top secret directive formally laid out American policy toward the Soviet Union by establishing that:

"U.S. policy toward the Soviet Union will consist of three elements: eternal resistance to Soviet imperialism; internal pressure on the USSR to weaken the sources of Soviet imperialism; and negotiations to eliminate, on the basis of strict reciprocity, outstanding disagreements."[22]

In furtherance of these goals, President Reagan ordered government agencies to perform a series of "tasks." These included:

- "To contain *and over time reverse* [emphasis added] Soviet expansionism by competing effectively on a sustained basis with the Soviet Union in all international arenas – particularly in the overall military balance and in geographical regions of propriety concern to the United States. This will remain the primary focus of U.S. policy toward the USSR."[23]

  Such a commitment, like the foundational precept of "eternal resistance to Soviet imperialism," was a new and radical idea – one that establishment figures often denounced at the time as irresponsibly provocative and dangerous. It was enshrined in the Reagan strategy's objective of rolling-back the Soviet Union.

- "To promote, within the narrow limits available to us, the process of change in the Soviet Union toward a more pluralistic political and economic system in which the power of the privileged ruling elite is gradually reduced."[24]

  This was a vital step in changing American strategy toward the Soviet Union because the new approach explicitly "recognizes that Soviet aggressiveness has deep roots in the internal system." In other words, the nature of Soviet behavior globally was directly related to the nature of the Soviet system and its guiding ideology of communism. Henceforth, the President ordered, U.S. policy would be guided by the principle that "relations with the USSR should therefore take into account whether or not they help to strengthen this system and its capacity to engage in aggression."[25]

To implement these tasks, NSDD 75 directed the U.S. government to: 1) support democratic forces within the Soviet Union; 2) highlight Soviet human rights violations; 3) strengthen U.S. broadcasting to the Soviet Union; 4) expose the double standards used by the Kremlin in dealing with its own domain and the capitalist world (the treatment of labor, policies toward ethnic minorities, the use of chemical weapons, etc.); and 5) prevent the Soviet propaganda machine from seizing the semantic high- ground in the battle of ideas through the appropriation of such terms as "peace."

Although not a part of NSDD 75, starting in March, 1983, President Reagan also assigned a high priority to "eliminating the threat of ballistic missiles" – the stated object of National Security Decision Directive 85.[26] This gave rise, in turn, to the establishment of the Strategic Defense Initiative (SDI), an ambitious plan for rendering such weapons "impotent and obsolete."

The Soviets, with their immense investment in nuclear-armed ballistic missiles perceived such a program as a potential game-changer, one with which – given U.S. technological advantages and resources – they were ill-prepared to compete. Combined with the larger Reagan Peace through Strength agenda, SDI helped demoralize Kremlin leaders and undermine their confidence in the USSR's military capabilities and prospects.

In short, President Reagan's strategy towards Soviet communism, which he expressly described as "one for the long haul," was instrumental in bringing about the collapse of the "evil empire" several years after he left office. That strategy's proactive, robust, and dynamic approach and key elements can – if adapted to countering and defeating today's totalitarian ideology, shariah, which some have called "communism with a god" – produce similarly salutary results against the Global Jihad Movement (GJM).

The following pages describe the nature and component parts of such an updated NSDD 75 game plan. Like President Reagan's original, the NSDD 75 2.0 strategy is rooted in an "exercise in competitive analysis." That analysis was performed in 2010 by Team B II, also a group of independent national security practitioners and other experts sponsored by the Center for Security Policy, whose report was published in a book entitled *Shariah: The Threat to America.*[27]

Members of the original Team B II, together with new contributors, have joined forces to develop and recommend this strategy for victory in this phase of the War for the Free World. In the following pages, they recommend ways in which NSDD 75 can be adapted and applied to defeating to today's ideological foe, the Global Jihad Movement and its ideology of shariah, through seven, complementary and mutually reinforcing initiatives:

1. **Restoring Peace Through Strength** as an instrument for countering kinetically, where appropriate and necessary, the Global Jihad Movement (including its Shiite components, led by Iran), while deterring actual and emerging threats from other quarters (notably Russia, China, and North Korea).

2. **Counter-ideological warfare** involving the explicit and public identification of the ideology of our enemies as evil and irreconcilably opposed to the universal truths, values, and freedoms upon which our Republic was founded. This component entails support for those within the Arab and Muslim world and those non-Muslims who are prepared to resist the GJM and oppose its shariah doctrine.

3. **Information operations** to counter jihadist propaganda and generate our own strategic communications to explain and defend the values

of the United States, that have served so well its own people and those of the Free World more generally.

4. **Intelligence operations** to subvert and neutralize the GJM's capacity to wage jihad here and against our interests elsewhere. Such operations must aim also to expose and disrupt the often hidden, ad hoc alliances between forces of the GJM and anti-American leftists of the communist and progressive camps.

5. **Economic warfare** to disrupt the financial support networks and revenue streams that facilitate the propagation of the ideology of jihad and enable its operations against us.

6. **Cyber warfare** both defensive and offensive to confront and engage the jihad and shariah networks that operate currently with far too much impunity across the Internet to conduct jihad operations that threaten us in each of the foregoing strategic battle spaces from disruption of critical infrastructure and the economic underpinnings of our societies to domination of the ideological and information spheres.

7. **Countering "Civilization Jihad" on the Homefront** to expose and defeat the program of penetration and subversion of U.S. society underway for five decades under the auspices of the Muslim Brotherhood in America.

KNOWING THE ENEMY

First and foremost, the United States needs to achieve a clear understanding of the enemy and its doctrine. That requires, in particular, clarity concerning the ideology its adherents call shariah, the jihad it impels and the various ways in which such warfare is being waged against us.

Just as with George Kennan's "Long Telegram," which explained the "sources of Soviet conduct" and paved the way for America's strategic response to the menace of expansionist Communism, today it is necessary to understand today the ideological sources of jihad conduct.

Because our self-declared enemies state that their fighting doctrine is based on the Islamic laws of jihad that derive from the shariah, those laws must be incorporated into any competent threat analysis. This simply follows Sun Tzu's primary rule to "know the enemy." Like the communists, al Qaeda, the Taliban, the Muslim Brotherhood and others have knowable threat doctrines. In fact, forecasting their activities is as simple as mapping their stated objectives to the doctrines they follow in conjunction with their known capabilities.

In particular, there are several key leaders, writers, and ideologues who laid the conceptual foundations for the violent jihad in which – to varying degrees – all Islamic supremacists engage today, be they members of the Muslim Brotherhood, al-Qaeda, the Islamic State (a.k.a. ISIS/ISIL), Boko Haram, al-Shabaab, or any other of the hundreds of groups engaged in terrorism in the name Allah. We cannot defeat these groups unless we know the works of these strategists intimately, as well as the geopolitical events that led to the rise in their influence.

When one assesses our shariah-adherent enemies in light of the Islamic doctrine they cite, it turns out that this doctrine *does* exist. Jihadis around the world consistently cite and act on its principles.

THE IDEOLOGICAL FONT OF MODERN JIHAD

As with the Bolshevik Revolution and the rise of Hitler, modern-day jihad is irrevocably linked to the events of World War I and their consequences. In an attempt to forestall the total dismemberment of the Ottoman Empire by the victorious allies, in part of his plan to create a modern secular state from the ashes of defeat, the Turkish premier, Mustafa Kemal Ataturk, officially dissolved the 1,100 year-old Caliphate – or theocratic empire of Islam – in 1924. Almost immediately, resistance to this decision grew across the Arab and Muslim world, which led eventually to the creation of the Muslim Brotherhood (MB) in Egypt in 1928.[28]

Founded by Hassan al-Banna, the Muslim Brotherhood was, and still is, predicated on the belief that Muslims must live only within the confines of governance run in accordance with shariah and that all other polities are anathema to Islam and must be subverted or destroyed. As such, the Brotherhood is the ideological grandfather to virtually all Sunni jihadist groups active today, and any organization, violent or not, which defines democracy as un-Islamic and which calls for the re-creation of the empire of Islam.

Banna's great feat was to create an organization that had a dual personality. On the surface, it would be openly active in providing services to the needy via schools, day care facilities, health clinics, and employment opportunities. Yet, under the surface, it created a vast network using a clandestine cell structure designed to spread propaganda and agitation to subvert the political systems of the Middle East and North Africa. This structure would also use violence as needed, including political assassinations, in order to eliminate political opponents, intimidate other critics and opponents, inspire militant loyalists, and help establish theocratic regimes, and eventually a re-born Caliphate.

While al-Banna was the central figure in the creation of the Brotherhood, it was another Egyptian, Sayyed Qutb who ultimately became the most important ideological influence within the Global Jihad Movement. A minor government official in the Ministry of Education, Qutb would be sent to the United States after World War II to study and observe American culture. In the two years he lived and traveled in America, Qutb came to the conclusion that the United States represents the worst of un-Islamic culture and that the United States must be destroyed as a nation if Islam is ever to regain its historical power and rightful place in the world.

As a result, his return to Egypt, Qutb wrote a slim volume, *Milestones*,[29] to explain why the West, and America as its leader, must be destroyed in a new jihad. Simply stated, there is no understanding Islamic terrorism and jihad without understanding the Islamic doctrines delineated in *Milestones*.

Qutb reasoned that the Muslim world had lost its way, was infected with Western mores and led by "false" Muslims. As a result the *ummah* – or global community of Islam – was again in a state of *jahiliyyah*, pagan ignorance of Allah, just as the nomadic tribes of the 7th century had been when Mohammad began to preach the Qur'an and establish what the Quran calls the perfect example for mankind on earth – the *Sunnah*. Qutb was explicit also in stating that at the time there existed not one truly Muslim state on earth. He exhorted his readers to understand that Islam is not a religion but a political movement whose goal it is to expunge ignorance of Allah from the world until the entire world lives under shariah.

With the 1979 invasion of Afghanistan by the Soviet Union, a new thinker provided a fresh and powerful theological case for jihad. Abdullah Azzam, a Palestinian Jordanian with a PhD in Islamic jurisprudence from the most important Sunni institution in the world, al-Azhar University in Cairo, declared that all Muslims must become jihadis. The logic of his *fatwa*, entitled *Defense of Muslim Lands*,[30] was that, since the Caliphate had been dissolved by Ataturk, the Muslim world had lost its commander-in-chief. In the interval, the infidels had invaded sacred Muslim territory and this demanded a jihad in response.

As a result, Azzam declared that, even in the absence of a Caliph, jihad is *fard ayn*, an individual and universal obligation incumbent on all Muslims. He created an organization in Pakistan to recruit Muslims from around the world and train them as guerrilla fighters to be deployed against the Soviets in Afghanistan. He hired a rich Saudi jihadi named Osama bin Laden as his deputy and their organization would later become al Qaeda, meaning 'the base' of the global jihad movement.

The third writer and strategist of notable influence with regard to the ideological character of the enemy threat doctrine is Brigadier S. K. Malik of the Pakistani Army. Also in 1979, Malik wrote a book entitled *The Quranic Concept of War*.[31] Malik's book combines analysis of military art with accounts of Mohammad's battles and theological argumentation on jihad. It has three key concepts:

The first is that war as an activity of mankind has nothing to do with the national interest, as Carl von Clausewitz, the renowned Prussian military theorist, maintained. Instead, war should serve one purpose and one purpose alone: the realization of Allah's sovereignty on Earth.

Second, when identifying how to attack the enemy, one should not look for "key vulnerabilities" or centers-of-gravity, since there is only one target that matters. That target is not even a physical one. In war, according to Gen. Malik, the only target that matters is the soul of the infidel whom one must convert or kill—a task made easier by first destroying the enemy's faith in himself and his cause.

Lastly, since the soul is the only target of import in war, Malik states that the most effective mode of war is terror.[32] It should be noted that this text by a general officer of the Pakistani Army, which justifies terrorism such as 9/11 or the Boston bombings as the best way to fight the unbeliever, was endorsed in its foreword and introduction by none other than the then-equivalent of Pakistan's attorney general and subsequently its president, General Zia ul Haq.

Although there are others one could mention, the three described above are the foundational strategists of the Global Jihad Movement. The essence of the enemy threat doctrine we therefore face is:

- Islam has lost its way and been subverted by the West. It must return to its true doctrine: shariah.

- The Caliphate must be re-established and expanded into a global entity.

- All governing systems that are not run in accordance with shariah must be subjugated or destroyed.

- Terror is the kinetic weapon of choice because it enhances the potential of a successful civilization jihad strategy by making Western/infidel governments more inclined to appease, tolerate and succumb to Jihadist elements.

Analysis that fails to account for these doctrines is academically and professionally unsound, if not dishonest. In the national security community, however, a reference for "political correctness" over accuracy has evolved to the point where models based on academic theories managed by outside "cultural advisors" are given credence over factual threat analyses. Some of the thought-leaders influential in reinforcing and promoting such analysis within the American defense, intelligence, national security and law enforcement communities have been individuals trained and mobilized by the Muslim Brotherhood and/or funded by shariah-adherent individuals, organizations and governments.

IMPEDIMENTS TO OUR KNOWING THE ENEMY

The jihadist thought-leaders are aware that the United States has abandoned Sun Tzu's dictum to know the enemy. They appear to have successfully calculated that they can win the war by convincing our national security leaders of the immorality of knowing the enemy they seek to engage, allowing the U.S. to squander its energy, resources and morale on fighting endless wars overseas, while waging their own pre-violent jihad

To divert attention from pre-violent forms of jihad already underway in 2001, they worked to keep the United States focused narrowly on al Qaeda, reluctantly supporting the "Global War on Terror" as long as the object was neutralizing bin Laden and his organization, but not their shared strategic objective of global shariah under a worldwide Caliphate.

The practitioners of pre-violent jihad conditioned American leaders to believe that too much focus beyond al Qaeda was misguided and even immoral. The advice of critics of the Global Jihad Movement, such jihadists argued, was motivated by racism, bigotry, "Islamophobia" and other forms of hate. Like the dogs in Pavlov's famous physiological experiments, U.S. policymakers and analysts learned to stay away from the objectionable.

Over time and with a new administration, the poorly termed "Global War on Terror" became, "Overseas Contingency Operations in Countering Violent Extremism." Note both the change and the continuity: What had been global was reduced to overseas (excluding jihad within the U.S.). What had been a war was reduced to "contingency operations"; any basis for a warfooting was gone.

The continuing theme, however, was the focus on the tactic of jihad: terrorism or violent extremism. Pre-violent jihad, including within the United States, was pushed even further off the target list.

At a minimum, national security decision-makers today consistently ignore, disfavor and even prohibit data that establishes the relationship between stated jihad doctrines and the strategies they enable. The ratcheting down of analytical standards has reached a point where they cease to meet minimum standards of professionalism. While it is not our fault that the threat we face identifies its doctrine along Islamic lines, it *is* our fault that we refuse to look at that doctrine when conducting threat analyses and that we anathematize those professionals who *do* study that doctrine with a critical eye.

The Muslim Brotherhood

A case in point is the Muslim Brotherhood. Contrary to what has become an institutionalized view within the U.S. government, the Muslim Brotherhood is *not* a moderate alternative to groups like al-Qaeda. Rather, the Brotherhood is the gateway entity from which these so-called "radical" groups have sprung and grow. Ideologically speaking, the Brotherhood facilitates the development of the jihadi from Da'wa practitioner, to political jihadi, and ultimately to violent jihadi.

In fact, while violent Jihad groups like al-Qaeda or Islamic Jihad may appear to be more violent and more obviously a threat, the Muslim Brotherhood is arguably far more dangerous. The Egyptians understand this from their own democratic experiment, as do an increasing number of other Arab states.

For example, in November 2014, the United Arab Emirates cabinet published a list of terrorist organizations that makes no distinction between groups like the Islamic State, al-Qaeda, Boko Haram, the Haqqani Network, Lashkar-e-Taiba, and Abu Sayyaf on the one hand and the Muslim Brotherhood on the other. Importantly, the UAE included by name the Muslim Brotherhood senior jurist Yusuf al-Qaradawi's Association of Muslim Scholars (IAMS or IUMS) and two U.S.-based organizations: the Muslim American Society (MAS) and a Hamas front operating in the United States, the Council on American Islamic Relations (CAIR)[33].

The U.S. Department of State asked the UAE for "clarifications" and European governments expressed indignation at the UAE report.[34] But other Arab countries added heft to the Emirati document. The Egyptian government quickly endorsed it, as did the 22-member Arab League. Thus the Arab League recognizes the Muslim Brotherhood as a common threat to each of their member regimes. This action of collective self-interest still provides an opportunity for U.S. agencies to work with the Emiratis and other Arab League members against the Brotherhood – but only if we have professionals at the operational and political levels who actually understand and stay focused on the threat.

We are on notice of the menace posed by the Muslim Brotherhood in America as well. As made plain by internal documents seized from the Brotherhood's U.S. arm and introduced into evidence during 2007 and 2008 trials in the *U.S. v. the Holy Land Foundation* case[35], the largest HAMAS terrorism-financing trial in the United States, the Brotherhood has been shown to have an explicit strategy to engage in "civilization-jihad" against the United States and the rest of Western civilization. The evidence in this case revealed that there exists in the U.S. today a massive jihad network which supports, finances, trains, and is raising a jihad generation right here in America.

The Muslim Brotherhood's stated purpose is sabotaging America and using America's free and open society to enable that sabotage, while operating as much as possible within the confines of the law to avoid scrutiny and interference. Our failure to know the enemy is, in part, evidence of the success of its civilization jihad operations.

A case in point: individuals and organizations identified in Brotherhood documents have also appeared in the federal government's investigative files, surveillance photos, audio recordings, and wiretaps, revealing them as aligned with the Muslim Brotherhood or as members of the organization. Yet, at the same time the U.S. government has also sought out Brotherhood-affiliated groups and individuals as cultural experts, and "community-outreach partners."

Far from being either moderate or an alternative to other, more immediately violent jihadis, the Brotherhood is committed to exactly the same goals as those it has inspired and enabled: the imposition of shariah worldwide and the establishment of a new caliphate to rule according to shariah. Its demonstrated ability to penetrate and subvert us makes its pursuit of these objectives via civilization jihad every bit as toxic as the violent kind.

Unfortunately, without characterizing the attitudes of all Muslims living in the United States, the public face of Islam here is increasingly that of the Muslim Brotherhood. More and more, Muslim communities in this country dominated by the Brotherhood and its dictates determine which Muslims are embraced by the White House, are selected to represent Islam in interfaith activities, or are allowed to provide the Islamic perspective in the media.

Muslims who do not want to follow the supremacist or jihadist elements of shariah have nowhere to go. They do not trust U.S. law enforcement and intelligence agencies because these entities are all known to work with the Muslim Brotherhood leaders and organizations. Recruitment of those who might be inclined to work against their jihad- and shariah-supporting co-religionists becomes extremely difficult as such Muslims are afraid to allow their true names and identities to be added to an official data base to which the Muslim Brotherhood has access.

American political leaders at all levels who refuse to recognize the nature of the Islamic supremacist threat and who make great efforts to appease jihadists are very discouraging to Muslims who reject such elements of shariah. Muslims in American communities who see a level of capitulation on the part of U.S. leaders are much more inclined to avoid entering any meaningful dialogue on how to reduce the threat of terrorism or to cooperate with law enforcement.

Indeed, particularly troubling is a fact understood by both friends and foes in the Arab world: the Muslim Brotherhood has achieved access to and influence over the highest ranks of the U.S. government. Examples abound.[36] Two are particularly noteworthy, however:

- Mohamed Magid, the imam of the All Dulles Area Muslim Society (ADAMS) Center (a complex of shariah-adherent mosques in Northern Virginia) and for several years the president of the Muslim Brotherhood's largest front organization, the Islamic Society of North America (ISNA), has advised President Obama, the Department of Homeland Security (DHS), and numerous other federal agencies and their leaders.

- Mohamed Elibiary is another prominent former member of the Department of Homeland Security's Advisory Council with ties to the Brotherhood. He is the founder and president of the Freedom and Justice Foundation[37/38] and Committee Chairman[39] and Board Member[40] of the Dallas-Fort Worth chapter of the Council on American Islamic Relations (CAIR).

Elibiary played a central role in events that led up to an October 2011 letter to the White House, in which elements of the American Muslim Brotherhood demanded that the White House remove from U.S. government training curriculum information and materials relating to Islamic-based terrorism, even insisting on firings, "re-training," and "purges."[41] The letter was addressed to then-Assistant to the President for Homeland Security and Counterterrorism, John Brennan.

Brennan, who would later become Director of the Central Intelligence Agency, answered the Brotherhood's demands by referencing the Obama administration's Countering Violent Extremism (CVE) narrative: "We share your sense of concern over these recent unfortunate incidents, and are moving forward to ensure problems are addressed with a keen sense of urgency."[42] Worse yet, he agreed on the necessity for the "White House [to] immediately create an interagency task force to address the problem."[43]

Talks between the administration and the Brotherhood took place at high levels, with the Director of the FBI going so far as to meet with the Brotherhood in February 2012[44] against the expressed directives of Congress.[45] More alarming, however, is how the FBI then proceeded to undertake the very purging of documents that the Brotherhood demanded[46] and the censoring of training materials at the FBI Academy in Quantico, VA. The Department of Defense followed shortly thereafter with a Soviet-style purge of individuals who trained officers and NCOs, along with disciplinary actions and re-education.[47]

Even these purges were not enough to satisfy the Brotherhood, a number of whose groups and associates issued a letter on 14 Aug 2014 to the Assistant to the President for Homeland Security and Counterterrorism calling for a second purge of materials/personnel and the demand for mandatory re-training of law enforcement exposed to fact-based training on the Muslim Brotherhood.[48]

It is instructive that Elibiary immediately condemned the 2014 designation by the UAE of CAIR and MAS[49] as terrorist organizations. He assured his Twitter followers, citing his own inside knowledge, that the United States counterterror community will ignore the UAE's action.[50] Endorsement of the UAE report by the entire Arab League, however, isolated Elibiary and CAIR, and serves as a basis for insisting that the United States not ignore the report's designation.

Elibiary was finally let go from his position at DHS following an investigation into allegations that he misused his security clearance to improperly access and use classified materials.[51] Presumably, his Twitter comments about the "inevitable" return of the Islamic Caliphate were considered problematic, as well.

The Organization of Islamic Cooperation

The nature and activities of one other jihad influence operation need to be understood and countered: the Organization of Islamic Cooperation (OIC). Its membership of 56 Islamic states plus "Palestine," includes a number of nations the

U.S. government insists are our coalition "partners." The OIC is sometimes described as a proto-caliphate.

The OIC wages what has been called "institutional jihad," especially through the entity's outsized influence at the United Nations (which is made possible by the sheer size of the organization's voting bloc and by the petrodollar wealth of a number of the OIC's members). It insists on presenting itself as the arbiter and authority for all Muslims on matters ranging from what constitutes international human rights to defining terrorism.

Although it was a Muslim Brotherhood entity, the International Institute for Islamic Thought (IIIT), that invented the term "Islamophobia," the OIC promotes it relentlessly as a means of dictating what can and cannot be said about Islam by non-Muslims worldwide and, thereby, shaping what non-Muslims can know and *do* in response to the jihad threat. Specifically, the organization has long sought to use international law to enforce what amount to shariah blasphemy laws in secular democracies.[52]

These initiatives amount to a coherent strategy to defeat America through agitation and propaganda campaigns that focus on the subordination of free speech to Islamic speech codes. In the United States, such subordination is unconstitutional. Thus demands for official enforcement of shariah blasphemy laws in the United States should be considered attempts to subvert or overthrow the Constitution.

Yet, during her tenure as Secretary of State, Hillary Clinton actually endorsed such curbs on speech.[53] In July 2011, Mrs. Clinton met with the Secretary-General of the OIC and personally committed the State Department's best efforts to secure the passage of a law restricting free speech, just as the OIC sought. She pledged that, even in the absence of such a statute, American citizens would be subjected to "peer pressure and shaming" should they choose to exercise their First Amendment rights of free speech in ways that give offense to Muslims as defined by the OIC.[54]

This appears to be an official view across the present administration. The top Justice Department official for civil rights echoed Clinton's pledge to the OIC. When the Chairman of the House Judiciary Subcommittee on the Constitution, Rep. Trent Franks, asked then-Assistant Attorney General for Civil Rights (now Secretary of Labor) Thomas Perez to affirm that the administration would "never entertain or advance a proposal that criminalizes speech against any religion," Perez refused to answer.[55] It is an ominous warning about First Amendment freedoms when the top Justice Department official charged with protecting civil rights refuses to respond to such a question. So was President Obama's declaration at the UN General Assembly in September 2012 that, "The future must not belong to those who slander the prophet of Islam."[56]

Such comments by top government officials reinforce concerns that since we do not know the enemy, we are unable to act effectively to defeat it. Increasingly do not even know ourselves as a nation, placing vague concepts of diversity, and tolerance of anti-constitutional extremism, above the Constitution itself.

To adopt and execute a strategy for doing the latter, it will be necessary to address the fact that senior leaders are ignorant of or willfully blind to the Islamic doctrine that confronts us. Not knowing this doctrine of shariah undermines our security. Ignorance kills. Ignorance in war brings defeat. America's current situation is tantamount to its Cold War leadership attempting to confront Soviet totalitarianism without any knowledge of the dictates of communism, the lives and examples of its ideologues, or the courage to declare that doctrine and those who subscribed to it enemies of the State. Not knowing the doctrine of shariah, the foundations upon which it is built, the ideologues who shaped and nurtured it, or its proponents today, undermines the security not only of America but the entire Free World and those who seek to be part of it. Ignorance kills. Ignorance in war brings defeat. Western Civilization cannot persist in such self-defeating behavior. The rest of this paper offers specific recommendations as to what we must do to turn defeat into victory.

RESTORING PEACE THROUGH STRENGTH

"Underlying the full range of U.S. and Western policies must be a strong military capable of action across the entire spectrum of potential conflicts and guided by a well-conceived political and military strategy. The heart of U.S. military strategy is to deter attack by the USSR and its allies against the U.S., its Allies, or other important countries, and to defeat such an attack should deterrence fail.

"Although unilateral U.S. efforts must lead the way in rebuilding Western military strength to counter the Soviet threat, the protection of Western interests will require increased U.S. cooperation with Allied and other states and greater utilization of their resources. This military strategy will be combined with a political strategy attaching high priority to the following objectives:

"Sustaining steady, long-term growth in U.S. defense spending and capabilities – both nuclear and conventional. This is the most important way of conveying to the Soviets U.S. resolve and political staying-power.

* * *

"Military Strategy: The U.S. must modernize its military forces – both nuclear and conventional – so that Soviet leaders perceive that the U.S. is determined never to accept a second place or a deteriorating military posture. Soviet calculations of possible war outcomes under any contingency must always result in outcomes so unfavorable to the USSR that there would be no incentive for the Soviet leaders to initiate an attack. The future strength of U.S. military capabilities must be assured. U.S. military technology advances must be exploited, while controls over transfer of military related/dual-use technology, products, and services must be tightened.

"In Europe, the Soviets must be faced with a reinvigorated NATO. In the Far East we must ensure that the Soviets cannot count on a secure flank in a global war. Worldwide, U.S. general purpose forces must be strong and flexible enough to affect Soviet calculations in a wide variety of contingencies. In the Third World, Moscow must know that areas of interest to the U.S. cannot be attacked or threatened without risk of serious U.S. military countermeasures."

-National Security Decision Directive 75

The United States is a nation with myriad interests facing global – and growing – threats to those interests. While the Global Jihad Movement (GJM) currently tops the list in terms of criticality, these threats are not confined to jihad and the U.S. must have the means to address them all, including those posed by peer-competitors like Russia and China. 21st Century threats increasingly are asymmetric in nature, dynamic in composition and 4th or even 5th generation in sophistication. A perception of U.S. weakness against any of them encourages all to chance levels of risk-taking that strength and deterrence could and should obviate.

For most of the post-World War II era, the U.S. has tried to hedge against dynamic adversaries and changing strategic circumstances by maintaining a formidable military. America's military doctrine was based on a powerful strategic deterrent with the capacity to project power decisively in more than one theater simultaneously. Following years of war in Vietnam and the hollowing out of the military that ensued in its aftermath, President Reagan made a centerpiece of his National Security Decision Directive 75 strategy the restoration of the U.S. military's capacity to secure "peace through strength."

Today, the U.S. faces peer adversaries, the increasingly capable forces of the GJM, and opportunistic alignments among them with a military that is arguably in even worse shape, with regard to both conventional and strategic nuclear forces, than the one that Mr. Reagan inherited.

At present, in a moment when hostile forces – including, but not limited to those posed by the Global Jihad Movement – are becoming significantly more capable, diverse and aggressive, America's doctrine might best described as hoping for peace despite weakness. Our military is incessantly being asked to accomplish ever-more-demanding global missions with ever-fewer resources.

At some point, it will no longer be possible to perform all these missions, particularly given changes in the character, technological sophistication and capability of current and prospective global threats.

The two alternatives would appear to be either: 1) Do *less* with less and run the risk of emboldening our enemies to still greater aggression against the United States and its interests; or 2) recognize the growing threats facing this nation and provide the additional resources necessary to maintain a military with the capability to address them, preferably through deterrence or, failing that, through the decisive use of force.

TAKING STOCK

A precondition for bringing to bear effectively the instruments of national power against today's totalitarian ideology and its adherents, as President Reagan did against the USSR and Soviet communists with his NSDD 75, is that we must know not only the enemy, but also *ourselves.*

The Kinetic War Against 'Terrorists' and 'Violent Extremists'

There are certain functions in countering and defeating the Global Jihad Movement, its ideology, and its enablers that only the U.S. military is capable of performing. We must, therefore, be clear about serious shortfalls in this regard.

The current approach to dealing with the global jihad threat has been characterized as using the military to "whack-a-mole." Military force is applied in small packages across the world in the hope of killing individual terrorists; forcing others to keep their heads down; and/or support coalition operations.

For instance, France's campaign against the Movement for Oneness and Jihad in West Africa (MUJAO) in Mali depended on U.S. transport and aerial refueling aircraft.[57] Nigeria's hunt against Boko Haram is being supported by U.S. surveillance drones.[58] U.S. Special Forces have been deployed to various African nations to combat jihadist organizations in those countries.[59] A large U.S. base has grown up in Djibouti to support operations against al-Shabaab in Somalia and Al-Qa'eda in Yemen.

The Obama Administration's strategy for dealing with the Islamic State has been more of the same: limited air strikes at great expense for questionable results.[60]

At the same time as the demand for whacking jihadist "moles" increases, the size of the military is shrinking. As a result, U.S. armed forces are being stretched to the breaking point. Of late, the Navy and Marine Corps have found it impossible to maintain the ongoing deployment of an amphibious ready group in the Mediterranean.[61] As a result, although various aerial and ground-based military assets were available within flying distance, none was deployed when jihadists attacked the U.S. mission in Benghazi on September 11, 2012.[62] Since then, however, the Marine Corps has been tasked to maintain a rapid response force in Southern Europe precisely for such contingencies.[63]

Recent air strikes against the Islamic State illustrate just how taxing it is for America's much-diminished military to mount even "limited" actions. What has gone underreported is the magnitude of the overall air operation entailed in conducting a relatively small number of bombing runs against IS targets in Iraq and Syria. This has required literally thousands of tanker flights, intelligence, search, and reconnaissance flights as well as flights by transport aircraft, in

41

addition to missions performed by aircraft maintainers, weaponeers, intelligence analysts, UAV operators, and communications specialists providing the accompanying support required to maintain even a limited number of actual air strikes.

In short, relatively small-scale counter-terrorist operations can require a disproportionate expenditure of military resources. They also impose wear and tear on scarce military resources, particularly surveillance platforms, aerial refueling aircraft, special operations forces, carrier battle groups and strike aircraft.

There is a debilitating impact on personnel as well. For instance, the U.S. Navy has been forced to extend the average length of aircraft carrier deployments from seven to nine months to provide minimum coverage of critical theaters. Such changes entail real hardship for the affected battle group's crews and their families.[64]

Another, longer-term cost is that arising from the diversion of the investment of scarce resources in the absolutely necessary modernization of aging platforms and the training for the sorts of missions would be required in the event of a confrontation with Russia or China.

The COIN Debacle

Arguably more debilitating even than the hugely costly misapplication of American military power against elements of the Global Jihad Movement to date, with few – if any – enduring, tangible benefits, has been the so-called Counter-insurgency (COIN) strategy that has governed, and contributed mightily to, that misuse.

The COIN strategy, particularly as implemented in Afghanistan, was predicated on the reckless misconception that "infidel" soldiers perceived by the native population to be occupying Muslim lands could "win the hearts and minds" of the population with a series of accommodations rooted in "cultural sensitivity," but total ignorance of the dictates of shariah.

Self-defeating aspects of this strategy included highly restrictive rules of engagement that prevented military personnel from learning and mastering cultural norms and ideologies for warfighting purposes, and from mastering jihadist ideology for the purposes of running divisive operations against the enemy.

The psychological operations career track remained a weak, obsolete and strategically ineffective discipline, pushed even further to the sidelines in part due to "cultural sensitivity" concerns and protests from Pakistan. These self-defeating measures not only exposed American personnel unnecessarily to harm and, in some cases, to loss of life. These accommodations were actually viewed as signs of submission by local populations and the jihadists that sprang from or otherwise operated among them.[65]

This harsh reality takes nothing away from the courageous and dedicated manner in which our nation's military adapted itself to execute COIN operations. Commanders at the tactical level might cling to memories of small temporary victories in the application of COIN operations in certain villages and cities where violence, for a time, was abated. The "Sunni Awakening" is one such event, whereby Sunni tribal leaders turned away from shariah-fixated jihadists to enable the temporary pacification of Al Anbar province in Iraq.[66]

For three years, though, Iraq's porous borders enabled the entry of thousands of foreign jihadists who demanded the loyalty of Iraqi Muslims[67] – claiming Islamic authority in accordance with shariah and carrying out the dictates of shariah[68] – including beheadings, murder, forced marriage and the use of unrelenting *shaheed* or martyr/suicide attacks against Muslims and non-Muslims alike.

Official lack of knowledge about jihad had enabled the Islamic Republic of Iran to infiltrate Iraq in the first place, beginning well before the March 2003 launch of Operation Iraqi Freedom, but building in the summer of 2003 to coordinate Shia mass street protests under the guise of religious pilgrimages.[69] Then, before any of Iraq's Sunni leadership began to disassociate themselves from these jihadists, not to mention the "Sacred Law" that impelled them, our own State Department facilitated the production of an Iraqi constitution that established Islam as the state religion and decreed that "no law may be enacted that contradicts the provisions of Islam."[70]

That American leadership could pursue such contradictory policies in its application of diplomacy and military force in both Afghanistan and Iraq is not surprising under the circumstances. Sending U.S. troops in harm's way while simultaneously hobbling their ability decisively to defeat the enemy with submissive COIN protocols and at the same time legislatively legitimating the very ideology that animates the enemy's jihad obviously is a schizoid way to prosecute a war. This sort of strategic and operational muddle, however, is the predictable result of our nation's failure to study that ideology so that the full potential of America's best generals and statesmen might have been permitted to prevail.

Persisting in such behavior is a formula for not merely needlessly sacrificing and demoralizing our men and women in uniform. It actually emboldens our enemies. And, as with the larger error of failing to know them, understand their doctrine, and pursue a comprehensive strategy for their defeat, COIN-driven practices make the chances of a Western victory in this War for the Free World much more remote.

THE MAGNITUDE OF THE PROBLEM

In July 2014, a bipartisan National Defense Panel (NDP) published a highly critical assessment of the adequacy of the Obama Administration's plans for America's military capabilities as defined by the Pentagon's Quadrennial Defense Review (QDR). The panel, which was co-chaired by former Clinton Secretary of Defense William Perry and former Central Command Commander Gen. John Abizaid, determined that, unless automatic, deep and across-the-board defense budget cuts known as "sequestration" are undone and additional resources provided to build a larger military and invest in more modern capabilities, "the Armed Forces of the United States will in the near future be at high risk of not being able to accomplish the National Defense Strategy."[71]

Whether the mission is addressing kinetic global jihad or deterring Russia and China, it is clear that the U.S. military today is too small, too old and too poorly maintained to provide for this nation's security. They are being sized effectively to deal, at best, with one adversary at a time.

After every major conflict over the past 70 years, American leaders decided they saw no future for conflicts and challenges involving a major land component. Over and over again, they were proved wrong, forcing the Department of Defense to undergo the costly and time-consuming process of rebuilding the land forces that had been allowed to deteriorate.

Too often, as epitomized by the ill-fated Task Force Smith in the early days of the Korean War, the Army has been required to throw inadequately trained and prepared ground forces in insufficient numbers into successive foreign conflicts in order to stave off defeat and buy the time necessary to build and deploy a capable Joint Force. The danger is that, in the future, we may not have the luxury of such preparatory time.

In its 2014 report, the National Defense Panel suggested that America must, instead, structure and maintain the forces necessary robustly to contend with multiple adversaries simultaneously:

> We feel it is imperative that as a global power with worldwide interests, the United States armed forces should be sized and shaped to deter and defeat large-scale aggression in one theater . . . while simultaneously deterring and thwarting opportunistic aggression in multiple other theaters . . . all the while defending the U.S. homeland and maintaining priority global missions such as global counterterrorism operations.[72]

Meeting this goal will be the more challenging in light of the dissipation of the technological superiority that was the hallmark of the U.S. military for the past sixty years. Shortly before his forced resignation, President Obama's Secretary of Defense Chuck Hagel warned that not only states such as Russia and China, but also rogue regimes like North Korea and *even terrorist organizations* were acquiring advanced technologies and weapons and building capabilities that were specifically intended to blunt our military's technological edge.

China, for example, has unveiled multiple stealth fighters that have likely been designed using highly classified information purloined from U.S. contractors through cyberespionage.[73] It has deployed a new generation of anti-ship ballistic missiles expressly designed to sink U.S. carriers and other warships.[74] China's armed services are also practicing amphibious assaults much more regularly, demonstrating a clear threat to China's neighbors. As a result, Secretary Hagel concluded:

> "Without our superiority, the strength and credibility of our alliances will suffer. Our commitment to enforcing long-established international law, rules of the road, and principles could be doubted by both our friends and our adversaries. Questions about our ability to win future wars could undermine our ability to deter them. And our Armed Forces could one day go into battle confronting a range of advanced technologies that limit our freedom of maneuver. This would allow a potential conflict to exact crippling costs and put at risk too many American lives."[75]

The U.S. nuclear arsenal, the central means of deterring direct attack on the United States and its major regional allies, is in accelerating decline. The United States is the only nuclear power (including rogue states such as North Korea and Iran) not systematically modernizing its nuclear weaponry and delivery systems.[76]

HOW TO RESTORE PEACE THROUGH STRENGTH

In short, the armed forces and, indeed, U.S. national security writ large, are at a crossroads. There are a number of steps that must be taken as part of a NSDD 75 2.0 strategy to assure that the military can deter and, if required, counter as it must present and future challenges.

Reconstitute National Security-mindedness

The American people and their elected representatives need to understand the broad responsibilities our military shoulders in the world, which include defending the American people, the U.S. homeland and American interests worldwide from myriad serious and sometimes deadly threats.

The public also needs to be given the facts about how large and capable a military is required in order to meet our vital national security interests and what it will realistically cost to acquire and maintain such a military. They must be equipped fully to appreciate the risks associated with reducing our armed forces to the point that they can only "do less with less." At the same time, the military must root out wasteful ways of doing business, and devise tactics and strategies that, wherever possible, will deliver more bang for the proverbial buck.

Employ the Military Sensibly

A new strategy for countering and defeating the Global Jihad Movement will involve important departures from recent practices. Among the necessary measures that will ensure the U.S. military is employed effectively in this fight are the following:

- Stop following submissive COIN/nation-building mantras. Decisive victories, achieved through an accurate understanding of the nature of the enemy and how it can be defeated – through the sort of comprehensive strategy proposed here – are far more likely to end the threat of shariah than doomed efforts to "win hearts and minds" through what our adversaries can only perceive as U.S. submissiveness. Our strategy should be modified to feature a robust ideological warfare outlook and capability to neutralize enemy hearts-and-minds campaigns.

- Abandon rules of engagement that are self-defeating. The American military must continue to work to minimize civilian casualties and collateral damage. But the first priority must be to accomplish the mission while assuring that those charged with doing so are not unnecessarily exposed to hostile fire or other risks.

- End the practice of relying upon so-called "allies" who are themselves led by jihad-supporting Islamic supremacist regimes. Such nations are, at best, playing double-games that imperil the security of American personnel and operations. At worst, they are enabling the very threat we confront: the shariah-driven global jihad.

Part of this problem may be solved by presenting such "allies" with the choice between supporting jihad or ensuring their own survival. Presenting such a stark choice, backed by the will to enforce it, could prove to be a cost-effective way for the United States to persuade some of the worst state sponsors of jihad to cease and desist (and reverse the damage) by appealing to their self-interest. Many of these regimes are fragile and fearful – vulnerabilities that the U.S. has failed to exploit.

Additionally, the U.S. should forge strong partnerships with our closest friends in Australia, Canada, Europe, Israel, New Zealand, and elsewhere who face the same threat from the same Global Jihad Movement. Standing with them — and, indeed, all who choose liberty — is the surest way to demonstrate the unified resolve of the civilized world to confront savagery and spare it the blight of shariah.

At a minimum, we must practice the most basic principle of a foreign policy rooted in the philosophy of peace through strength: It should be far better to be an ally of the United States than its enemy. Only by conducting our affairs in this fashion do we have stand a chance of decisively thwarting the efforts of aggressive jihadists, and their enablers, to increase the number and lethality of our foes and neutralize or eliminate our friends.

Rebuild America's Military

The first priority as part of a broader strategy to wage war decisively against our enemies is to stop the hollowing out of our armed forces. This will require the following measures:

- Remove the boot of sequestration from the Pentagon's neck. The military services have already made an enormous contribution to restoring fiscal sanity in Washington. If the next round of sequestration is allowed to come into effect in FY 2016, it will do enormous damage to military capabilities and readiness.

  As former Secretary of State Colin Powell warned in another context, "You break it, you own it." The new Congress must take the lead in sparing the defense budget from further, devastating cuts. The Department of Defense, however, must address and eliminate where they exist wasteful practices and abuse of taxpayer resources.

  While reining-in runaway government spending is of vital importance to the future of the Republic, everything should *not* be on the table when it comes to deficit reduction and balancing the budget, most particularly the common defense of the American people. The idea that Pentagon spending, now only 20 percent of all federal spending and less than four percent of GDP, should continue to bear 50 percent of the cuts is absurd, reckless and unsustainable.

- Remediate the decline in readiness across the military. This means ensuring that there are no "hangar queens," ships tied up to the dock, aircraft or vehicles rendered inoperable due to a lack of spare parts. It means also enhancing training, particularly for high-end missions, which would necessitate providing additional flying hours for pilots and crews.

- Place the Navy's shipbuilding budget on a path towards a fleet of no fewer than 350 ships. As part of this effort, take the nuclear ballistic missile submarine replacement program out of the Navy shipbuilding budget where it swamps other programs.

- Protect key Air Force modernization investments, specifically the F-35, the new strategic bomber and the KC-46 tanker. In addition, the future of airborne intelligence, surveillance and reconnaissance (ISR) is at risk with the proposed retirement of the U-2, the aging of the JTARS and AWACS fleets and the failure to prepare adequately for operations in contested air and space domains.

- Halt the decline in the size and combat potential of the Army and Marine Corps. The Army's Active Component cannot be allowed to shrink to the size of a forlorn hope, attempting to stem the tide of an enemy's advance until the Reserves show up. If the military is to have the flexibility and depth required to be able to execute its part of this NSDD 75 2.0 strategy, a regular Army of no fewer than 450,000, with improved logistics and transportation capabilities, will be necessary to assure the capacity quickly and ably to respond to new threats. The size of the Marine Corps must be maintained at least at 174,000. In addition, the fleet of amphibious warfare ships must be increased to a minimum of 38 ships.

- Rebuild our nuclear deterrent forces. The U.S. nuclear enterprise has been more or less frozen in amber since it was last comprehensively modernized by President Reagan. The credibility, and therefore the effectiveness of our strategic and tactical deterrents have been jeopardized by the nation's failure to replace aging air-, land- and sea-based delivery systems.

Worse yet, the weapons such bombers, missiles and submarines carry are beyond their designed service life, obsolescing and in need of replacement by safer, more reliable bombs and warheads. Indeed, none has been subjected to the ultimate test – an underground nuclear detonation – since 1992. That is true even of weapons that have had some of their components replaced with potentially unpredictable implications for performance.

At a time when every hostile nuclear weapon state is modernizing and increasing the lethality of its arsenal, the United States must upgrade its deterrent forces across the board and do the same for the industrial and testing complex that is essential to its future viability.

- Deploy an effective national missile defense. President Reagan understood the necessity of defending the American people, not simply avenging their annihilation. To that end, he commissioned a Strategic Defense Initiative with the express purpose of providing comprehensive anti-missile protection for the United States and her allies including, among other things, highly efficacious space-based defenses.

With the rapid proliferation and increasing sophistication of ballistic and cruise missile threats, it is imperative that the United States once again pursue the development and deployment of such defenses. These should include the emplacement of sensors and anti-missile systems capable of protecting the nation from several threats that could emanate from the south – including electromagnetic pulse (EMP) attacks delivered by ballistic missiles launched from ships in the Caribbean or Gulf of Mexico, Iranian land-based missiles based in Venezuela or North Korean satellite-based fractional orbital bombardment – an axis of attack against which America currently has no protection.

- Exploit advanced technologies to maintain American military superiority. Public comments from a number of senior defense officials make clear they believe that, if the military is to remain strong, it is imperative that investments in critical technologies be increased. Areas for particular consideration include: electronic warfare, cyber defense, nuclear weapons, directed energy, unmanned vehicles and secure access to space.

- Treat industry as a partner and not as an adversary in forging a strong defense. Republicans have been united in their drive to get government to stop treating business as an adversary and to implement pro-growth policies. The new majority in Congress needs to apply this same logic to the defense sector. The overgrowth of regulations, audits, and reporting requirements needs to be severely pruned back. Wherever possible, best commercial practices, including in accounting standards, need to be applied to defense contracts.

- While not generally regarded until now as a national security priority, the growing threats to the most critical of U.S. critical infrastructures – our bulk power distribution system (popularly known as the electric grid) – also demands attention. Jihadists (among others) now have, or soon will, the ability to engage in physical sabotage, cyber attacks or the use of nuclear weapons to generate far-reaching electromagnetic pulses capable of destroying high-voltage transformer substations – the effectively irreplaceable backbone of the grid.

For example, one of the most dangerous of jihadist operations, the Islamic Republic of Iran was recently discovered to have used cyber attacks to gain access to the control systems of the U.S. electric grid for over *two years*.[77] Another revelation in the past few weeks is no less worrying: As the mullahs approach the endgame on their decades-long quest for nuclear weapons, we have learned that their strategic doctrine includes references in twenty places to the offensive use of EMP.[78]

A further consideration is that – even if none of these actions is taken against our grid by an enemy, we are certain to see our bulk power system subjected to devastating levels of electromagnetic energy from another source: the Sun. Roughly every 150 years, an extremely intense solar storm hits the earth. The last one occurred 155 years ago.[79] If it happened today, its effects would be roughly comparable to those of a high-altitude EMP attack.

Should the grid be taken down either way, power could be denied to large areas of the country *for years*, with truly cataclysmic effects on our population, economy, society and environment. This must be prevented as a matter of the utmost urgency.

Therefore, an NSDD 75 2.0 strategy must mandate the coordinated efforts of federal, state and local authorities, working with the private sector – which owns 85% of the electric grid, to develop and implement a plan for the triaged protection of this critical infrastructure, starting with its most essential substations, control facilities, power generation sites and dedicated telecommunications assets.

Providing for America's security must once again be assigned the priority, resources, training and leadership commensurate with the perilous circumstances of present phase of the War for the Free World. By so doing, it will be possible for the U.S. military and other elements of our national and homeland defense to perform the functions required of them by the NSDD 75 2.0 strategy: dealing decisively with today's threats and deterring tomorrow's.

WAGING COUNTER-IDEOLOGICAL WARFARE

U.S. policy must have an ideological thrust which clearly affirms the superiority of U.S. and Western values of individual dignity and freedom, a free press, free trade unions, free enterprise, and political democracy over the repressive features of Soviet Communism....Building and sustaining a major ideological/political offensive which, together with other efforts, will be designed to bring about evolutionary change of the Soviet system. This must be a long-term and sophisticated program, given the nature of the Soviet system.

[The U.S. must] prevent the Soviet propaganda machine from seizing the semantic high-ground in the battle of ideas through the appropriation of such terms as "peace."

–National Security Decision Directive 75

Just as in the Cold War, it is imperative that the United States and the Free World use techniques that are suited to defeating an ideologically motivated enemy. This will require an expanded understanding of the need for, the nature of and the means to execute an effective communications strategy to counter jihad and shariah messaging.

THE NATURE OF THE CHALLENGE

The war that has been forced upon our civilization is seen by the enemy primarily as ideological warfare, which manifests itself in the U.S. as influence operations calculated to penetrate and subvert the pillars of American society: academia, faith communities, government institutions, the legal system, media, politics, and society in general.

Yet, our entire government structure is focused on the kinetic war – shootings, bombings, kidnappings and other acts of "terrorism." We are not only failing to win in the information battle-space, we are not even engaged in that space because we do not understand it is the enemy's self-identified main focus of effort. Everything our enemies do is meant to affect our psyches at the level of beliefs, emotions and thoughts as the entryway to affecting our actions.

Even when we *do* attempt to engage in the information battle-space, we fail because we have neglected to learn the enemy doctrine. Enemy plans for jihadist violence here in the U.S., as well as Afghanistan, Iraq, Syria, and elsewhere, are important to the enemy, but secondary to the greater world-wide ideological struggle in the information domain.

Our failure to understand this and to know the enemy doctrine cripples our ability to engage the enemy where he fights his main battle. Therefore, over time, the enemy dislocates our people from their faith in the bedrocks of our civilization – Judeo-Christian values, liberal democratic principles and the U.S. Constitution – and simultaneously provides ideological encouragement to millions of potential supporters among targeted Muslim populations through indoctrination in shariah, participation in jihad and the promise of eternal paradise.

Soviet communism was a serious threat to the Free World, but its lack of "promise" to broad masses of people – not to mention economic bankruptcy and the Free World's dedicated fight against it – led to its collapse. Meanwhile, over nearly 1400 years, shariah ideology has conquered multiple major world empires and today stands virtually unchallenged in the ideological battle space. The survival of the Free World requires that this situation change drastically.

Strategic Communication

The purpose of U.S. government strategic communication should not be simply to inform people around the world, but to persuade them (by means rational or kinetic, as required) of the superiority of Western principles and society. Such communication entails more than the transmission of words and ideas. It should also involve operations within the information battlespace executed for their psychological effects on others.

Specifically, an updated NSDD 75 strategy must be supported by strategic communications, the principal purpose of which is to suppress the will of others to act in ways contrary to American interests. Because this conflict is ideological – a belief system that governs the human psyche – the battle space must be understood to include the environment in which that psyche resides: the human mind.

Well-established techniques for carrying out these sorts of official strategic communications – such as information operations and psychological operations (re-named "military information support operations" by the U.S. government in 2010) -- are today limited in their application to advancing the mission of the armed forces. As a result, they are, with rare exceptions, tactical/operational in focus and reactive in practice.

The Policy Problem

Worse yet, the Obama administration's increasingly institutionalized secularist – if not *actively pro-Islamic* – policies have largely prevented the U.S. government from engaging in strategic information operations aimed at exposing and undermining the supremacist doctrine of shariah and the terrorism it commands.

Such policy guidance is evident in innumerable statements by senior American officials involved in counterterrorism issues. To cite but two recent examples:

- Notwithstanding an explicit commitment in President Obama's address to the nation in September 2014 – in which he told the American people that targeting the Islamic State's "ideology" would be one element of his new counterterrorism strategy[80], Richard Stengel, a former *Time* magazine reporter and the current Under Secretary of State for Public Diplomacy, declared that the administration would not attempt to wage a war of ideas against the Islamic State. The reason, according to Stengel: the Islamic State is "bereft of ideas."[81]

- In October 2014, Dr. Quintan Wiktorowicz, the former Senior Director for Global Engagement at the National Security Council and the Obama administration's key theorist for counterterrorism, made an astonishing announcement. He asserted that the U.S. Constitution's "establishment clause" – intended by the founders to prevent the establishment of a state religion – precluded the administration from using information operations or other means to deal with the problem of Islam's jihad ideology. Wiktorowicz contended that "while the government has tried to counter terrorist propaganda, it cannot directly address the warped religious interpretations of groups like ISIL because of the constitutional separation of church and state."[82]

These and similar propositions leave us defining enemies by their methods (e.g., as "violent extremists"), rather than by their strategic goals. Pursuant to shariah, the latter entail, in particular, seeking to destroy this country, including via subversion by attacking the Constitution of the United States, and to overthrow the international order, to our national detriment. Counter-factual nostrums by American officials are evidence of mindsets and policy direction that are further undermining the already ineffective contemporary U.S. strategic communications, information operations and psychological warfare, such as they are.

The Anti-American Mindset

Even absent the hamstringing effects of policies presented as "politically correct," but actually submissive to supremacist Islamic information dominance, the task of promoting the United States and protecting its interests in the information battle space has been complicated by one other factor: the low regard among American elites and others in the general population for this country and its founding principles. This level of disregard is evident in many government bureaucracies that have been influenced for decades by leftist/liberal/progressive ideologues. It is reflective of an American culture that shares with this nation's critics the view that we have been too powerful, domineering and indifferent to the legitimate rights/aspirations of others.

The upshot has been little – *if any* – official effort being made to minimize the damage done to U.S. prestige and influence by: the ineffectually contested, and ongoing, expansion of al-Qa'eda and the ominous rise of the Islamic State; the U.S. failure to render appreciable support to Iranian opposition efforts while projecting an all-too-accommodating willingness to accede to the nuclear weapons ambitions of the regime in Tehran; the disastrous Russian "reset"; and the anemic Asia "pivot." As a result, the perception has taken hold in many quarters that America is no longer the strong, reliable and confident leader of the Free World.

The present U.S. approach leaves us with few options but to target kinetically individual combatants and commanders at the tactical/operational level. We have failed to pursue, let alone employ widely, measures designed to neutralize pro-shariah thought-leaders, jihad ideologues and others at the strategic, ideological level and to attempt to alienate their followers from them.

In the decades since Iran first launched its part of the global jihad against us in 1979, we have demonstrably seen more enemies enter the fight than have been eliminated. In particular, the virtually exclusive focus on physically targeting "violent extremists" has conveyed to other, more influential and strategically consequential leaders of the shariah-advancing movement that we will neither target nor otherwise seek to render them ineffectual. Our submissive unwillingness to confront them gives credence to their belief that "Allah wills" the victory of their ideology over ours, further emboldening them.

AN ALTERNATIVE COUNTER-IDEOLOGICAL STRATEGY

The needed alternative has the following characteristics:

- Our main strategic objective against the Global Jihad Movement is not to kill every believer and practitioner in that movement.

- Rather, our principal strategic purpose is to deprive adherents to shariah's offensive, supremacist aspects of the will to be practitioners of that doctrine and the jihad it impels.

- Many who embrace the ideology of global jihad will never relinquish their allegiance to it. Such adversaries can, nonetheless, still be targeted with effective counter-ideological operations. If properly executed under a coherent strategy, such operations can, at a minimum, sow confusion, disinformation and dissension among jihadist ranks.

- To the extent, however, that it *is* possible to diminish the appetite of Islamic supremacists to embrace this threat doctrine – for instance, by imposing pressures that give rise to intolerable changes in their psychological and even physiological environments, an opening is created. We can then move in with additional political, informational and ideological warfare tools useful for destabilizing our foes' ideological base. In some cases, we may even be able to alter their worldviews.

A prerequisite for this sort of counter-ideological strategy to be effectively formulated and implemented is that the U.S. national security leadership must establish a fact-based training curriculum in the core Islamic canon that forms the basis of the enemy's belief system (a.k.a. the enemy threat doctrine) and serves as the wellspring of its zeal for jihad: Quran, hadiths, Sirat and shariah. Absent such fundamental knowledge of the enemy's ideology, no counter-ideological strategy is possible.

Historical Precedent

Warriors and civil and religious leaders have engaged in ideological/psychological warfare to achieve strategic ends since Classical times and across cultures.[83] Long before President Reagan promulgated NSDD 75, the U.S. government embraced this set of capabilities as part of its strategic warfare against Soviet Communism in the late 1940s and early 1950s. Presidents Truman and Eisenhower explicitly described it as "psychological strategy."

This facet of U.S. Cold War strategy was outlined for President Truman in a document known as NSC-68, drafted by a team under Paul Nitze in 1950 and formally adopted in 1951. NSC-68 provided the foundational national definition of a strategic ideological warfare threat and laid out an American strategic response. Importantly, NSC-68 described the conflict with communism in terms of saving "civilization."

NSC-68 viewed the strategic ideological conflict with the Soviets in four equal components: (1) military, (2) economic, (3) political, and (4) psychological.

President Truman sought to coordinate psychological operations globally through an inter-agency Psychological Strategy Board (PSB), but limited the role as an aid to operations, and not as part of an integrated strategy.[84] President Eisenhower, arguing that psychological warfare could not be conducted independently of official policy and actions, abolished the PSB as new agencies like the CIA and US Information Agency were stood up, transferring the Board's psychological warfare roles to a new coordinating group.

Unfortunately, subsequent presidents almost never have used the term psychological strategy and, with the notable exception of Ronald Reagan, have not assigned a priority to employing it for counter-ideological purposes. While the United States has continued to evaluate conflicts in military, economic and political terms, it no longer officially considers the strategic psychological component.

The Current Imperative

The timing for a course correction in this regard is opportune. Heretofore, one of the major handicaps the United States has faced has been the lack of reliable allies in the Muslim world, who are much better culturally positioned and materially resourced to serve as effective messengers to target audiences – were they, in fact, motivated to do so. Such allies have more streamlined means of policy execution than the U.S. government and have more cultural and doctrinal credibility as effective messengers to various audiences globally.

Recent developments in Egypt, the United Arab Emirates, and even the Arab League suggest a broadening and deepening opposition to the Global Jihad Movement. These developments may represent an opportunity to weaken the jihad narrative – particularly that of the Muslim Brotherhood – and place the United States in a better position to wage an international campaign to attack that movement. At the same time, we need to remain cognizant that deep-seated traditions, domestic political considerations, external rivalries and emerging threats to such regimes may impel them – when push comes to shove – to recoil from any meaningful renunciation of the supremacist Islamic shariah doctrine or its obligation to jihad.

For whatever opportunity these developments may actually hold, this is the time to restore the ideological/psychological facet of strategy to equal standing with the military, economic and political ones. That is the case not only because of the importance of ideological imperatives to our jihadist enemies. It is also due to the fact that the military, economic and political facets are powerfully influenced by the psychological, as it is the psychological dimension that tends to govern the effectiveness of the other three.

By assigning due emphasis to conceptualizing and executing a counter-ideological/psychological warfare strategy to fight and win a long-term conflict against shariah-driven global jihadists, we may be able to: avoid as much as possible direct armed contact; wear-down and demoralize the enemy; and inspire and hearten our allies, friends and neutrals who are also being targeted by Islamic supremacism.

In short, by properly bringing to bear effective counter-ideological strategic influence in furtherance of our death struggle with the Global Jihad Movement, we will stop unilaterally disarming in this battle space. The effect will be greatly to enhance our performance in all others, notably by increasing the effectiveness of training, education, operational and strategic doctrines and strategic planning.

Managing Effective Ideological/Psychological Warfare

An interagency mechanism should be charged with operationalizing and overseeing the targeting for the nation's strategic communications and psychological warfare. In light of the urgent need for such a capability, the federal government can quickly create an ad hoc entity, one modeled loosely on the Reagan-era "Active Measures Working Group."

This U.S. Information Agency-led team was formed during the Reagan administration to expose and otherwise counter Soviet disinformation operations as executed through what the Soviets called "active measures."[85] Directed by the Soviet Communist Party International Department and executed by the KGB, active measures included strategically designed disinformation and propaganda, agents of influence, use of international front organizations and co-optation of independent organizations, infiltration of enemy institutions and support for terrorism, guerrilla warfare, and political assassinations. Active measures operated seamlessly in support of Soviet diplomatic and military strategy.

The White House established the Active Measures Working Group to coordinate an interagency approach to the spectrum of political warfare tools that the Soviets employed. Some of Moscow's effective and inexpensive tools included the forgery of documents attributed to senior U.S. officials and launching political warfare campaigns opposed to U.S. strategic nuclear modernization, ballistic missile defense, foreign military bases and aid to countries under attack by Soviet-backed insurgencies.

One of the enduring forgeries that haunts the United States even today is the KGB disinformation asserting the U.S. government manufactured HIV as a pathogen to target black Africans and people of African ancestry. Although the supporting documents were subsequently debunked as forgeries, the themes reemerged in 2014 amid false reports that the Pentagon engineered the Ebola virus for the same purpose. Such messaging could hardly be more cynical, in view of the Kremlin's own massive biological warfare program that includes weaponized Ebola.

The new interagency mechanism must practice strategic communication as much more than effective, planned use of information, arguments, and facts to persuade others. Under a properly designed and executed ideological/psychological warfare strategy, the same mechanism would coordinate messaging and actions to send a message and modify a target's will and behavior. The operations of this interagency group should be conducted in the classified realm.

Equipping Ourselves to Secure Information Dominance

To realize fully the benefits of such a new counter-ideological strategy, the United States must dramatically enhance its instruments for securing and exercising "information dominance" in the main battlespace of the Global Jihad Movement and against peer competitors like Russia and China. Achieving such dominance will be made all the more challenging due to the massive and sustained investment made by our jihadist enemies and other adversaries in the infrastructure and instruments of propaganda and the practice of strategic communications.

Of particular concern is the progress made in recent years in this regard by jihad-financing regimes like Qatar's (the sponsor of Al-Jazeera's worldwide television propaganda operations) and jihadist organizations like al Qaeda and the Islamic State (notably, through an increasingly sophisticated use of social media). In addition, America also confronts China's announced "Three Warfares" – legal, psychological, and media warfare.[86] These are now advanced by the PRC's Xinhua propaganda-purveying news service and the ostensibly private information technology conglomerate, Alibaba.

For its part, Vladimir Putin's regime is employing with considerable effect state-controlled propaganda instruments like "Russia Today" and KGB-style information attacks and disinformation.[87] The insidious influence operations of the so-called "Iran Lobby" and the Muslim Brotherhood among senior national security decision-makers receives scant notice from, let alone effective counteraction by officials responsible for counterintelligence and information warfare. Oversight committees of the Congress have, to date, provided no perceptible challenge to this practice.

In fact, it is no exaggeration to say that, in the face of such threatening information operations, the United States has basically disarmed. As discussed above, that has been true at the policy level, with what amounts to official prohibitions on the understanding of our global Jihad enemies and waging counter-ideological war against them. Such unilateral disarmament is also evident at the level of capacity to wage counter-ideological warfare.

Dismantling the Mechanisms for Information Operations

Matters have been made much worse by the dramatic degrading of official U.S. instruments for conducting strategic communications critical to information dominance.

For most of the Cold War years and subsequently until 1999, successive federal law and presidencies made it the mission of the U.S. Information Agency "to understand, inform and influence foreign publics in promotion of the national interest, and to broaden the dialogue between Americans and U.S. institutions, and their counterparts abroad." In its heyday, the USIA's budget was over $2 billion annually. The agency and two independently operated "surrogate" radios, Radio Free Europe and Radio Liberty (RFE/RL), played a key role in President Reagan's strategy for destroying the USSR.

In 1999, however, Congress and the Clinton administration shut down the USIA. Its functions nominally were assumed by a State Department Undersecretary for Public Diplomacy and Public Affairs. Within Foggy Bottom, however, more powerful bureaus with competing agendas have rendered this secretariat basically useless as a tool of competent public diplomacy, let alone for decisive pro-American information strategy.[88]

The Obama administration has, in addition, largely neutralized several platforms that have, in the past, been instrumental in telling the United States' story to the world and countering hostile powers' information operations against us.

For example, the Voice of America (VOA) was once a vital source of accurate information about the United States and the wider world for millions of listeners around the globe. Today though, the organization lacks leadership, direction and resources and much of its once-formidable infrastructure for reaching audiences in key nations and regions has been dismantled. Congress bears a major share of responsibility for this situation insofar as the VOA's Broadcasting Board of Governors, while independent of the Executive Branch, lacks the legislative mandate required for adequate funding and strong leadership.

Worse yet, its Persian News Network has been accused of such a systemically pro-Tehran-regime bias that a bipartisan group of congressional members has demanded that the State Department launch an investigation.[89] Other "surrogate" broadcasting operations – meant to complement the work of VoA, but be independent from it – such as Radio Free Europe/Radio Liberty, Radio Free Asia, Radio Marti and Radio Sawa, are far less effective than was RFE/RL during the Cold War, even though they have dedicated and competent professional staff in many of their units.

Needed: New Information Warfare Capabilities

What is required now, as part of a new counter-ideological strategy squarely focused on the Global Jihad Movement and adversaries like China and Russia, is a fresh national resolve and capacity to promote America to foreign audiences. We must be able to neutralize wherever possible anti-U.S. propaganda – including disinformation, influence campaigns and other "active measures" – being intensively conducted by our actual or undeclared enemies.

As in the past (notably, under NSDD 75), the information warfare mission should be performed and funded as a priority by the federal government. Given the importance of this mission to our security and the needed, new strategy for enhancing it, however, in the absence of such governmental leadership, consideration must be given to establishing alternative, private sector vehicles for waging this form of warfare.

The specific goals of such efforts must be: countering enemy propaganda about America; de-legitimating those who engage in it and other hostile actions against us; and empowering those overseas who share our values and enemies to join forces with us and become more effective in promoting the former and defeating the latter.

Specific Lines of Attack

Among the specific focuses for such a new information warfare capability to counter shariah and other enemy threat doctrines should be:

- enhanced dissemination via social media networks of truthful information about America and the lies being promoted about her, done in a strategic, imaginative, flexible and operationally nimble fashion;

- the development of expanded infrastructure and other means of reaching audiences in critical parts of the world, including: the Middle East; Central, South and East Asia; Africa and Latin America. At a minimum, there should be no further dissipation of existing U.S. government short-wave and other broadcasting operations in these regions;

- enlistment of Hollywood in efforts to produce films engendering a more accurate image of this country and its enemies (a task that will be made more difficult, but more necessary than ever in the wake of North Korea's efforts to prevent the public release of "The Interview); and Hollywood's increased income stream from growing audiences in China, where U.S. movies must receive approval from the regime; and

- a challenge to the Orwellian manipulation of language that is an important instrument employed to America's detriment by jihadis, the left, and others hostile to this country and the Constitution upon which it was founded and the Constitution upon which it was founded.

Unfortunately, as the murderous jihadist attack on *Charlie Hebdo* thrust into the international spotlight, an effective counter-shariah campaign against such hard targets also will have to acknowledge that a truthful portrayal of core American principles such as equal rights, individual liberty and government under rule of man-made law by consent of the governed will be portrayed as offensive to shariah-adherent Muslims for whom such concepts are anathema. Therefore, merely conveying the truth about our democratic, liberal, Western society will hardly suffice for the jihadist target audience. Rather, an effective information warfare campaign against such populations must include offensive operations including, where necessary, character assassination, deception, dissimulation, distortion, false flags and ridicule.

The United States has tried, with dismal results, to wage war against jihadist elements without utilizing effectively either defensive or offensive strategic communications and ideological/psychological techniques informed by a realistic understanding of the larger movement and its doctrinal roots. We have allowed the means of waging such warfare to atrophy or be eliminated outright.

It is high time that such techniques and capabilities be resuscitated and utilized as integral parts of a strategy modeled after National Security Decision Directive 75.

MOUNTING EFFECTIVE INTELLIGENCE OPERATIONS

This military strategy will be combined with a political strategy attaching high priority to the following objectives:

- *Creating a long-term Western consensus for dealing with the Soviet Union....*

- *Building and sustaining a major ideological/political offensive which, together with other efforts, will be designed to bring about evolutionary change of the Soviet system....*

- *Effective opposition to Moscow's efforts to consolidate its position in Afghanistan....*

- *Blocking the expansion of Soviet influence in the critical Middle East and Southwest Asia regions....*

- *Maintenance of international pressure on Moscow to permit a relaxation of the current repression in Poland and a longer-term increase in diversity and independence throughout Eastern Europe.*

- *Neutralization and reduction of the threat to U.S. national security interests posed by the Soviet-Cuban relationship....*

–National Security Decision Directive 75

Successive policy failures related to the resurgence of jihad and shariah, the ideology that impels it, have severely undermined U.S. national security over a period of decades. During the Obama presidency, these trends have accelerated and worsened. U.S. intelligence agencies have contributed significantly to these policy failures in large measure because they fail to think in strategic terms in the conduct of collection, analysis, operations, and counterintelligence.

Additionally, U.S. counterintelligence does not consider infiltration of government agencies or co-optation of federal employees to be a counter-intelligence concern if those acts are not carried out by formally structured intelligence services of foreign governments. Infiltration, for example, by the Saudi government's Ministry of Religious Affairs, or by the Muslim Brotherhood, is not regarded as an intelligence operation that requires monitoring or countering.

It is our conviction, however, that the current debilitated condition of U.S. intelligence operations is due more to a failure of will than lack of capability. With renewed resolve and a rejuvenation of traditional clandestine tradecraft skill sets – including more strategic collection, more strategy-minded analysis steeped in enemy threat doctrine and more willingness to utilize of operational tools that include deception, false flag, and influence operations, pursued with cunning and tenacity – the U.S. Intelligence Community can take its rightful and needed place at the leading edge of the counterjihad campaign.

The intelligence community's approach to jihad and shariah has mirrored the tendency of the foreign policy establishment and the mainstream media to dismiss and downplay the threat posed by Islamic supremacism. Public clarity about that threat has also been compromised by the distortion of intelligence analysis and terminology used to describe Islam, jihad, and shariah to conform to the Muslim Brotherhood's calculated corruption of both the narrative and professional training programs, and the Obama administration's policy assumptions. Examples include:

- U.S. intelligence agencies have adopted the White House's blacklisting of the terms "radical Islam," "Jihad" and "homegrown terrorist."[90]

- On February 10, 2011, Director of National Intelligence James Clapper said at an open House Intelligence Committee hearing that the Muslim Brotherhood was a "largely secular group," that "eschewed violence" and had "no overarching agenda, at least internationally."[91]

- U.S. intelligence and law enforcement agencies insist that the 2009 Ford Hood massacre was an act of workplace violence and not an act of jihad. This requires ignoring relevant facts, including: Maj. Nidal Hasan was known by the FBI to be in e-mail communication with and taking instruction from al-Qa'eda in the Arabian Peninsula ideologue and recruiter Anwar al-Awlaki. The shooter cast himself as a "Solider of Allah" and had repeatedly warned comrades of his obligation under shariah to kill those who were preparing to oppress Muslims. And Hasan shouted "Allahu Akbar" – the Muslim war cry required to be uttered in the act of jihad – as he murdered and wounded dozens of servicemen and women. The 86-page After Action Report (AAR) dubbed '*Protecting the Force: Lessons from Fort Hood*,' contains not a single entry of the words "jihad" or "Shariah" within its text.[92]

- Under the sway of Muslim Brotherhood agents of influence, in 2011 and 2012, the intelligence community and the rest of the U.S. national security establishment conducted purges of their official training curricula and lexicons to remove all references, course materials, and instructors that would appropriately link Islamic doctrine, law and scripture to terrorism conducted by jihadists.[93]

- In September 2012, CIA Deputy Director Michael Morell and CIA analysts politicized talking points prepared for Congress on the attacks against the U.S. mission in Benghazi by asserting that they were spontaneous demonstrations in response to an anti-Muslim video and not a pre-planned jihadist operation. [94] This memo deliberately ignored a report by the CIA Station Chief in Tripoli that stated the attacks were "not an escalation of protests."[95]

U.S. INTELLIGENCE AND THE COUNTER-IDEOLOGICAL STRATEGY

The point made earlier bears repeating in the present context: The U.S. government cannot defeat our enemies abroad or defend the homeland against them as long as it refuses to know who they are or understand either their objectives or strategy for achieving them. The nation must repudiate the sorts of inaccurate threat assessments described above and end the practice of requiring the intelligence community and other national security agencies – and, for that matter, the American people – to operate on the basis of such self-deluding and - defeating characterizations of the threat.

A new strategy modeled after the Reagan NSDD 75 approach must, among other things, direct U.S. intelligence agencies to: produce honest, insightful, and pull-no-punches assessments of this threat; engage in better intelligence collection against the entire spectrum of jihad targets, whether of the violent terrorist or stealthy infiltration type; and conduct effective counterintelligence and covert action to defeat the Islamic supremacist enemy.

Specifically, a multidisciplinary approach to counter-intelligence must be employed aggressively to gain entry to and ultimately control the enemy's intelligence and international propaganda apparatus, even as that enemy has done to us. Once inside those intelligence and propaganda apparatuses and the enemy's decision-making loop, counterintelligence methods must be applied to blind him, confuse him, deceive him, and prod him into fatal errors that we should be prepared to exploit and shape.

Situational Awareness

U.S. intelligence agencies must be directed to end the practice of performing threat assessments through an inaccurate, "politically correct" prism in favor of unvarnished realism about the nature and agenda of the forces of jihad and shariah. At a minimum, this will require that:

- Intelligence analysts and managers must be able to orient on Islamic supremacism as a broad-spectrum, doctrinally-based, global threat whose vanguard includes extensive jihad forces, both violent and stealthy. They must be both allowed and encouraged to recognize that some of both are currently operating within the United States, including within the U.S. government and Intelligence Community.

- Intelligence analysts and managers in particular must be free to address the implications of shariah, Islam's supremacist ideology, with its obligatory legal system and dictates for governing all aspects of its adherents' lives – and, the lives of all others, as well. Attempts to intimidate, suppress or otherwise discourage such honest analysis and thinking should be punished professionally and, as appropriate, investigated as potential enemy infiltrations of our national security community.

- Intelligence analysts and mangers must be allowed to operate on the basis of derivative realities:

  o Terrifying violence is a central feature of the jihad required by shariah.

  o The Muslim Brotherhood's *modus operandi* in the United States and elsewhere in the West (known as "civilization jihad") is *not* a non-violent and preferable alternative to such jihadism. Rather, it is *Dawah*, a *pre*-violent means of creating conditions under which the infidels' submission is assured.

  o The jihadists are making effective use worldwide of Islamic front groups and franchises for both subversion and, where practicable, for coordinated or at least synergistic violence. And

○ The jihadists are imaginatively and adaptively employing both traditional and asymmetric warfare techniques. These include political warfare and information operations to enable the spread and triumph of shariah internationally.

Organizing for Victory

Senior intelligence officials must, with the full backing of the president, develop and implement analytical, intelligence collection and covert action initiatives against jihad targets worldwide. This will entail plans for comprehensively gathering from human as well as other intelligence sources and methods. It will also require thorough and sustained analysis as part of the "preparation of the battlefield" for the various elements of this strategy (notably, political warfare, economic warfare, and information operations).

These initiatives must be able to call upon the resources and support of the entire government. Therefore, they require direction and the active support of the White House. Plans for their actualization must include benchmarks to measure successful implementation. This will entail, among other things, the intelligence community being tasked to produce a series of national intelligence estimates on the evolving threat posed by adherents to shariah and the status of their efforts to impose it worldwide via jihad.

Reorienting U.S. intelligence agencies to help defeat aggressive, supremacist Islam and its shariah ideology will take more than a new strategy and sustained presidential leadership. Because this policy shift is certain to be opposed by (among others) intelligence careerists, successfully implementing it will require principled presidentially-appointed officials with the strong backing of the White House. Above all, the intelligence community must be returned to a professional status that focuses on the mission of intelligence in defense of national security and no longer is permitted to engage in partisan policy debates.

In this regard, it is important to remember that NSSD-75 was bitterly opposed by some CIA analysts who claimed it reflected the tendency of President Reagan and CIA Director William Casey to exaggerate the Soviet threat. Although Messrs. Reagan and Casey were proven right after the Cold War ended, resistance to the President's strategy for defeating the Soviet Union was so strong that it led to constant, unfounded complaints that Director Casey "politicized" analysis of the USSR. It subsequently caused several CIA analysts to testify publicly against former Casey deputy Robert Gates during his 1991 confirmation hearing to be the CIA Director.

A similar bias was evident during the George W. Bush administration in the frequent efforts of CIA officers to undermine Bush policy, often by leaking classified information to the press. A September 2004 *Wall Street Journal* editorial condemned this conduct by intelligence professionals by calling it "the CIA insurgency."[96] Other intelligence officers who had downplayed the threat of China in official thinking, tried to intimidate analysts from exercising their best sound judgment on Chinese capabilities and intentions and sought to influence national policy[97], were later found to have maintained improper and even illegal contacts with the Chinese intelligence services. One senior officer was convicted.[98]

The Reagan administration was more successful than that of Bush '43 in overcoming the resistance of hostile CIA professionals to its policies. This was due in no small measure to the fact that President Reagan had in William Casey a principled and energetic Director of Central Intelligence who was committed to implementing aggressively the President's policy to defeat Soviet communism and who had his boss' full and unequivocal support in doing that. To accomplish this task, Casey carried out a revolution within the CIA by taking back control of the organization from the careerists, installing his own people in senior positions and – for a time – changing the culture of the Agency. In retrospect, Casey is widely regarded as one of the most effective directors in CIA history.

Resistance by intelligence officers to a NSDD 75-style strategy for countering the Global Jihad Movement can be expected to be particularly strenuous. In addition to the aforementioned bias within the intelligence community, we confront the cumulative effects of countless careers invested in and built advancing the policies of willful blindness about shariah and accommodation of its adherents pursued to date. Then, there is the problem of decades of successful infiltration of the intelligence community, as well as other parts of the U.S. government, by Muslim Brotherhood, Iranian and fellow traveling agents of influence.

For these reasons, an intelligence revolution similar to what occurred during the Reagan era is needed to engage U.S. intelligence agencies to implement a new strategy for defeating the Global Jihad Movement and countering its animating ideology For these reasons, an intelligence revolution similar to what occurred during the Reagan era is needed to engage U.S. intelligence agencies to implement a new strategy for defeating the Global Jihad Movement and countering its animating ideology of shariah. It may even be necessary to create the equivalent of a new OSS (Office of Strategic Services), the small, secretive wartime intelligence unit established by President Franklin D. Roosevelt in 1942.

Bureaucratically, of course, such a step would be very difficult today, but if the U.S. intends to get serious about fighting the Global Jihad Movement, such a black operations unit – agile, liberally-funded, with broad authority for self-initiative that incorporates the skill sets of clandestine intelligence operatives, counterinsurgency special forces capabilities, plus cyber, financial forensic, linguistic and socio-cultural expertise may be the only way to get the job done.

As noted above, any intelligence reform surely will be made more difficult than the implementation of NSSD 75 was because the U.S. intelligence community is much larger and more bureaucratized than it was in the 1980s. Although this is in part due to the natural growth of government bureaucracies, it also reflects the deleterious effects of changes wrought in response to the Intelligence Reform and Terrorism Prevention Act (IRTPA) of 2004. IRPTA imposed additional layers of bureaucracy that have made the U.S. intelligence community less efficient and more risk-averse.[99]

Fully enlisting the intelligence capabilities of this country in a counter-ideological strategy to defeat the Global Jihad Movement will first require the president to name a National Security Adviser to head the National Security Council who fully understands the threat of shariah, has the confidence of the president and the authority to act to make such changes as are required to implement the Commander-in-Chief's direction. Similarly minded and principled individuals must be named to head the other agencies responsible for elements of U.S. intelligence (including the Office of the Director of National Intelligence (ODNI), the Central Intelligence Agency, the Defense Intelligence Agency, and the Departments of Defense, State, and Homeland Security).

All of these top officials must be committed not just to lead their agencies to combat the Islamic threat agenda, but also to deal effectively with internal resistance within their agencies to this effort. This means they must shake up their respective bureaucracies and name outside people to key positions. Even without the establishment of a new OSS, at a minimum, such personnel and bureaucratic changes should include:

- Appointing competent, non-career experts to top positions in the National Counterterrorism Center (NCTC), the CIA Counterterrorism Center and the Department of Homeland Security (DHS). In particular, the NCTC director should come from outside the intelligence community.

- Creating a Director of National Intelligence Mission Manager to coordinate the intelligence community's analysis, collection, and covert action against the Global Jihad Movement and its animating ideology, shariah.

- Creating a National Intelligence Officer for Global Jihad to be charged with monitoring this movement and its supremacist threat doctrine. This NIO would be responsible for the production of relevant national intelligence estimates. Such estimates should be subject to outside reviewers, but not by those associated with the Muslim Brotherhood or Iranian front organizations in America.

- Reprioritizing counter-intelligence functions with a mandate to root out and otherwise neutralize Muslim Brotherhood, Iranian and similarly motivated influence operations and those conducting them.

- Creating new offices and centers in the ODNI, CIA, DIA, DHS, and FBI to prioritize intelligence analysis of this issue and encourage collaboration between intelligence analysts and intelligence collectors and covert action. This could include a "CIA Counter-Jihad Center."

To be sure, personnel and bureaucratic changes along these lines will be fiercely resisted by intelligence careerists, the news media, political partisans and Islamist front groups and their allies, all of whom will attempt to generate popular opposition to them. It is predictable that the opponents' narrative will be that such restructuring and appointments, like the overall strategy itself, unfairly target Muslims and pose threats to the civil liberties of other Americans. The White House and its appointees in the intelligence community must be prepared to hold the line, including by reassigning or firing officers who undermine this policy – especially officers who speak to the news media without authorization.

Reorienting Intelligence Collection

The success of a counter-ideological strategy will also require reorienting U.S. intelligence assets and capabilities to prioritize collection against the Global Jihad Movement. Such efforts should include:

- Mandating new intelligence collection requirements against both Islamic supremacists and all other forces that aid, abet and support the spread of their ideology and influence. Such requirements should be coordinated with the National Security Council and regularly reviewed and, as necessary, updated.

- Threat-based training courses for intelligence collectors that include a focus on the threat doctrine - shariah.

- Reestablishing FBI collection and surveillance against all individuals, facilities or groups operating in support of Islam's jihad and shariah agenda within the United States, whether in Muslim communities and mosques or elsewhere among sympathetic fellow travelers. This tasking should apply to those clearly tied to violent jihad as well as those promoting *Dawah*, or pre-violent civilization jihad.

- Improving intelligence-sharing and coordination between U.S. intelligence agencies and, as appropriate, with foreign intelligence and security services on the Global Jihad Movement and its ideology.

- Making better use of state and local counterterrorism fusion centers as force-multipliers to conduct and defend intelligence collection operations against individual jihadis who may be American persons operating within the homeland in support of the global jihad agenda. The U.S. needs more of these centers and the intelligence community should work more closely with them.

- Assessing how to salvage NSA collection programs relevant to countering the Global Jihad Movement that were damaged or compromised by Edward Snowden's leaks. This initiative must include consultations with the intelligence oversight committees to win their support for shoring up wherever possible and otherwise reconstituting these critical capabilities.

Conducting Intelligence Operations against the GJM and Shariah

Taking a page out of the U.S. intelligence community playbook in implementing NSSD 75, a central element in executing a new counter-ideological strategy against the Global Jihad Movement must include robust covert operations so as to, in President's Reagan's words, "contain and reverse over time" the expansion of shariah and the Islamic supremacism it mandates. The express object must be to counter, divide and undermine the GJM and the threat it poses worldwide.

This "intelligence war" against jihad and shariah will require that the president approve, at the earliest opportunity, comprehensive findings authorizing aggressive covert actions. Such clandestine efforts should include:

- Neutralizing leaders, operatives and ideologues of the GJM – preferably through capture and incarceration – to allow for interrogation about their secretive organizations and activities.

- Using the Guantanamo Bay detention facility for this purpose.

- Targeting the worldwide financial activities, bank accounts and funding sources of the jihad enemy, across the economic spectrum. (See in this connection the following section on the economic warfare elements of this strategy.) This should include undermining shariah finance and shariah-inspired sovereign wealth funds, as well as countering the economic warfare of the global Jihads and their state-sponsors.

- Undermining Islamic supremacism by identifying, exposing and countering its doctrinal foundations through information warfare (see the foregoing counter-ideological warfare elements of this strategy) to undermine its support and counter its propaganda on the internet and in the media.

- Lending both official and non-attributable support – including funding, technological assistance, training, and weapons – to individuals and groups worldwide that are demonstrably willing to fight the Global Jihad Movement and its shariah agenda.

- Intensifying surveillance, special operations and all manner of kinetic strikes against jihad infrastructure and personnel.

- Implementing aggressive cyber warfare efforts to target jihad computers and communications, including infiltration of the jihadist online presence to disrupt, hack and manipulate its communications, proselytizing and training.

- Finally, if the Intelligence Community cannot get a grip on protecting its most important secrets and keeping them off the front pages, none of these other measures will succeed. Ensuring no more Edward Snowdens means overhauling the security clearance process and reinstituting an emphasis on defensive counterintelligence.

As with President Reagan's strategy, employing intelligence capabilities in the pursuit of both accurate situational awareness and political warfare objectives will not be without either controversy or setbacks. They are, nonetheless, essential as part of a truly comprehensive approach to countering successfully an ideologically driven adversary.

CONDUCTING ECONOMIC WARFARE

- *U.S. policy on economic relations with the USSR must serve strategic and foreign policy goals as well as economic interests. In this context, U.S. objectives are:*

- *Above all, to ensure that East-West economic relations do not facilitate the Soviet military buildup. This requires prevention of the transfer of technology and equipment that would make a substantial contribution directly or indirectly to Soviet military power.*

- *To avoid subsidizing the Soviet economy or unduly easing the burden of Soviet resources allocation decisions, so as not to dilute pressures for structural change in the Soviet system.*

- *To seek to minimize the potential for Soviet exercise of reverse leverage on Western countries based on trade, energy supply, and financial relationships.*

–National Security Decision Directive 75

THE THREAT ENVIRONMENT

In 2005, a Jordanian journalist scored an important interview with Seif al-Adl, the al-Qaeda military commander in Iran, which was published by the German online outlet *Der Spiegel* in August of that year. According to this enemy leader, the forces of Islamic jihad planned to conquer the West and establish a Caliphate with a Seven-Phase Plan.[100]

Starting with the 9/11 attacks that he called "The Awakening" phase, al-Adl laid out successive stages of a plan that called for the "collapse of the hated Arab governments" between 2010-2013, followed by the declaration of the caliphate between 2013-2016. What is so striking about this interview is how, in hindsight, it has proven remarkably predictive.[101]

In recent years, relatively pro-Western and secular regimes in Turkey, Lebanon, Tunisia, Libya, Egypt and, most recently, Yemen have been replaced, at least temporarily, with ones more sympathetic to – if not actually part of – the Global Jihad Movement. And in 2014, the newest manifestation of that movement, the Islamic State, has declared a new Caliphate.

As images of atrocities and human rights abuses by the Islamic State spill across computer and TV screens around the world, awareness is spreading that amputations, beheadings, crucifixions, executions of prisoners and sex slavery are intrinsic to Islamic law, or shariah. What is less well understood, however, is that the ultimate objective of jihad and those who wage it is the universal imposition of shariah across the entire world. What the civilized world considers atrocities are, in fact, also calculated means to an end for the forces of jihad.

Barbaric punishments and savagery not only comprise core elements of shariah, but are utilized to strike terror into the hearts of non-Muslims, so as to accelerate their loss of will to fight and readiness to accept subjugation under Islamic Law. Economic warfare attacks at the hands of jihadists can also contribute greatly to the conditions needed to achieve this end-state.

THE NATURE OF ECONOMIC WARFARE TODAY

While top ranks of the U.S. national security establishment – including the Secretaries of Defense and State, the Chairman of the Joint Chiefs of Staff, and the Intelligence Community – have acknowledged the kinetic threat posed by the Islamic State here and abroad, none appears to understand how this vanguard of the Global Jihad Movement, let alone the rest of it, endangers Western *economies*, as well.

Unfortunately, the economic warfare threat is not confined to the exhortations of the likes of Anjem Choudary, a grandstanding Islamic supremacist based in the United Kingdom, who has explicitly called for the economic exploitation of the infidel (or *kuffar*) at the street level: "The normal situation is to take money from the *kuffar*. You work, give us the money."[102]

Neither is al Qaeda, which has explicitly called for economic jihad against the U.S., Israel and the West on a broad *macro* level, the only cause for concern in this domain.

The truth, whether it is acknowledged or not, is that the West has been engaged for decades in a global economic war with shariah-adherent governments, their oil and other enterprises and sovereign wealth funds. The menace posed by this facet of the GJM has, to varying degrees, been compounded by counterpart efforts in this domain from the likes of China, Russia and North Korea.

Matters have been made worse, however, by a newly established force in the Global Jihad Movement that is positioning itself to engage in such economic jihad operations: the Islamic State. This al Qaeda offshoot is extremely well-funded, with a diversified base of revenues that reportedly amount to millions of dollars a day. It is said to be building a massive war chest from all manner of criminality, extortion, hostage-taking, oil proceeds and taxation. It is also establishing connections to sophisticated drug cartels around the world, including in the Western hemisphere.[103]

IS bankers and portfolio managers clearly understand financial markets and appear to be advancing longstanding Muslim Brotherhood and al Qaeda plans to infiltrate the financial services industry. This process is already well underway in the form of Shariah-Compliant Finance (SCF).[104]

Today, with IS as well as the Islamic Republic of Iran and other elements of the Global Jihad Movement ready to collaborate in assaults on our economy, with or without the assistance of hostile non-Muslim regimes, we must undertake both defensive measures and adopt offensive economic warfare techniques to counter and, wherever possible, defeat such enemies.

The Global Jihad's Economic Target Set

In particular, al Qaeda has exhorted its followers to include targeting oil facilities, oil fields, shipping, the U.S. dollar, and the Western financial infrastructure. The American forces who killed bin Laden recovered writings from his hideout describing his strategy to attack these infrastructures, but U.S. intelligence was slow to inform the targeted companies. Osama bin Laden lived long enough to see his goal achieved of oil shooting up to $100 a barrel.[105]

The October 2014 issue of al Qaeda's online magazine, *Resurgence*, laid out the strategy in some detail. It urged jihadists to sabotage Western businesses in the global oil, mineral and fishing industries. The magazine further urged Muslims to avoid using Western banks and financial markets, and instead reinstate gold, silver, and other commodities as the basis of an Islamic financial system intended ultimately to collapse the American dollar.[106]

It is worth noting that all of these measures are listed in the 2005 *Der Spiegel* al Qaeda timeline. In fact, the correlation is almost perfect. And while the 2014 establishment of the Caliphate by IS may have preceded, rather than followed, the AQ plan to collapse the U.S. dollar, the overall jihad against the economic underpinnings of Western civilization remains on track.

Nation State Economic Warfare

Of course, economic jihad is not confined to covert activity by terror groups. Even the so-called "moderate" shariah-adherent states have engaged in economic warfare against the West. One prime example was the 1973 Arab Oil Embargo which was directly followed by a stock market collapse and near-depression.

In effect, we used the weapon of lower oil prices ourselves during the Cold War. A key part of President Reagan's NSDD 75 strategy for destabilizing and destroying a Soviet Union hugely dependent – as is the Kremlin today – on energy exports involved enlisting the Saudis to glut the market with oil.

That still-potent weapon is once again being wielded today by Saudi Arabia, this time against *us*. The Saudi Arabian Oil Minister, as reported in *Arab News*, recently declared outright the intention to "combat (the) U.S. shale boom."[107] This is significant because, according to the American Petroleum Institute, without American shale development, the price of oil would have risen as high as $150/barrel in 2013. In addition, the economic benefits of that boom have been enormous, contributing more than half-a-million jobs during 2013 according to some estimates, roughly a quarter of the 2.2 million total jobs added that year.

In other words, the Saudis have targeted one of our most important industries responsible for a good amount of our economic growth. Their stated goal now is to drive down the price of oil to make the shale industry collapse so they can regain control of oil and thus "the weapon of oil" which they can extract at a fraction of the cost of oil from shale.

It is important to note, however, that lower oil prices based on Saudi production provide benefits as well. Lower prices weaken Russia, threaten the regimes of Iran and Venezuela and provide at least a temporary financial benefit for oil-importing nations, including the United States. In other words, the ominous nature of this particular economic attack on our longer-term energy security is somewhat obscured by what are at least short-term strategic windfalls.

Economic Warfare Has Already been Used Against Us

There is reason to believe that economic warfare techniques besides oil price manipulation have already been used to attack this country. In *Secret Weapon: How Economic Terrorism Brought Down the U.S. Stock Market and Why It Can Happen Again*, author, Chartered Financial Analyst and former Pentagon consultant Kevin Freeman revealed shocking evidence that America's enemies unleashed economic war against our financial markets starting on September 11, 2008. Vulnerabilities in the U.S. financial system, including its failure to protect against such tactics as oil manipulation, bear raids, credit default swaps, rogue trading, and naked short trading contributed to the ability of this country's enemies – including, it appears, al Qaeda and other jihadists – to cause the collapse of such financial giants as the American Insurance Group (AIG), Bear Stearns, and Lehman Brothers.

The continuing refusal of the U.S. government to confront honestly what happened in 2008 – and who was responsible – means that our financial system remains vulnerable to enemies with the means, motive, and opportunity to do us harm and are increasingly emboldened by our repeated demonstrations of weakness.

Shariah-Compliant Finance

One of the most formidable economic weapons such forces are bringing to bear is shariah-compliant finance. SCF is possibly the world's fastest-growing industry. Its most prominent feature is the professed prohibition of taking or charging of interest. In practice, however, this industry reflects the time-value of money in various financial schemes and marketing sleights of hand. Another hallmark of SCF is its refusal to invest in products or activities deemed *haram* (or impure/impermissible) under shariah, such as alcohol, gambling, pork products, and infidels' military industries.[108]

Less well known in the non-Muslim world, though, is that fact that shariah-compliant finance has been developed over a period of decades by the leadership of the Muslim Brotherhood specifically for the purpose of waging financial jihad against, and ultimately destroying, the lynchpin of Western economies: capitalism. Because scarcely any Westerners in governmental agencies and financial institutions trouble themselves to learn about the economic jihad aspects of shariah-compliant finance, there has been a widespread embrace of this practice and its alluring promise of access to immense Middle Eastern sovereign wealth funds.

Our situational awareness of the actual threat posed by shariah compliant financial operations is exacerbated by the clever marketing of this industry as nothing more than an innocuous Muslim alternative to the supposed immorality of the free market capitalist system. Throw into the mix the contention that shariah's adherents are entitled to use such a parallel financial system as an extension of their constitutionally protected freedom of religion, and you have a formidable Trojan horse inside Wall Street's gates.

In fact, SCF is not only being insinuated into Western capital markets an alternative Islamic financial system intended to undermine and replace our own. It also contains within its shariah code a disguised method to *fund* jihad.

For Muslim individuals and enterprises to be "shariah-compliant," they must pay what amounts to an obligatory annual tax called *zakat*, which is collected and administered by shariah-adherent Islamic authorities. Again, non-Muslims are led to believe that *zakat* is nothing more than a Muslim's constitutionally protected religious duty to provide charity for the needy. Yet, although much of the annual tax revenues collected through *zakat* payments indeed is distributed to charitable causes, according to shariah, a fixed percentage (12.5%) must be channeled to jihad.

Moreover, by requiring equity partner ownership instead of interest-based loans in nations where a few families own all the shariah finance institutions, SCF effectively makes a small aristocracy the principal owners of all new ventures. This exacerbates a major source of the failure in economic development and lack of opportunity in such countries.

When combined with overlapping shariah compliance boards among competing institutions – boards that demand and obtain near-total visibility into Western bank and client operations – the result is often institutionalized corruption, conflicts of interest and serious security flaws. The U.S. Treasury Department has, nonetheless, actually promoted shariah compliant finance as a means of repatriating petrodollars under both Republican and Democratic administrations.[109]

This is all the more outrageous insofar as the Internal Revenue Service and Congress may be interested to know that SCF products such as home loans actually deprive the IRS of interest and capital gain revenues. The U.S. Tax Code, as currently written, is not equipped to deal with SCF products in a fair and equitable fashion, with one result being that low-to-middle income taxpayers wind up paying more in taxes, interest and capital gains than they would if they used SCF home mortgages. The same government officials who claim an inability to act against jihadist ideology by invoking the establishment clause are ignoring the favoritism the Tax Code provides Shariah-Compliant Finance.

Last but not least, both al Qaeda and the Islamic State are among those pushing for the use of a gold-backed dinar and abandonment of the U.S. dollar in the oil trade. IS leader Abu Bakr al-Baghdadi reportedly intends to begin minting gold, silver and copper coins for use by his self-declared caliphate. It is unlikely the caliphate's new monetary system will take hold anywhere except territory under its control, but in terms of symbolism, IS seeks in one more way to demonstrate the global jihadists' opposition to, and determination to destroy, the prevailing international financial system.[110]

WAGING OUR OWN ECONOMIC WARFARE

Taking a page from the Reagan NSDD 75 playbook, economic warfare must once again be a preeminent part of our strategy, this time for the purpose of countering and defeating the Global Jihad Movement. Specific steps that must be pursued as high priorities include the following:

- Constricting the principal source of revenues for jihad – i.e., vast petrodollar transfers from Western nations to OPEC states that are the wellsprings of support for its jihad expansionism and the supranational enabler of that enterprise, the Organization of Islamic Cooperation. Burgeoning energy supplies within this country and in our neighbors to the north and south offer opportunities for leverage that can be used to defund OPEC and bankrupt others dependent on its underwriting of jihad and those who sponsor it.

  For example, we can exploit natural gas and also natural gas-derived methanol as transportation fuels, allowing the sector that is the principal U.S. consumer of foreign oil – and the nation – to be weaned from what remains of their dependency on foreign supplies (currently some three million barrels per day).

  An additional benefit from establishing that most cars operating today can utilize alcohol-based fuels, as well as gasoline, would be to enable more than 100 countries around the world to produce such fuels from their own feedstocks (namely, such carbon-rich resources as natural gas, coal, switch grass, trash, wood chips, biomass, etc.) The practical effect of such energy independence – not just in this country, but world-wide – would be to break the back of the OPEC cartel.

- Disrupting the flow of illicit oil revenues from jihadist entities like the Islamic State. It would seem natural for OPEC members to support such a strategy, given that some of them (especially the Saudis) are being targeted by the Islamic State. The willingness even of some who fight against the Islamic State to buy its oil under the table at deeply discounted prices, however, underscores the unreliability of the OPEC members and reinforces the point that destroying their cartel should be a strategic priority for the United States.

- Treating shariah-adherents in the global financial markets and international trading system the same way as jihadists of other stripes. This would mean stigmatizing and isolating them, not enabling and rewarding them. Specifically, we must reverse the present practice of accommodating and even *encouraging* shariah-compliant finance. SCF must be recognized and exposed for the jihad vehicle that it is, taxed in manners not currently addressed by federal and state tax codes, legally banned for U.S. companies, in violation of the U.S. Criminal Code with respect to material support for terrorism and disrupted worldwide by whatever means possible.

- Exposing shariah-inspired sovereign wealth funds as instruments of financial jihad. This will require, among other things, taking on Gulf Cooperation Council (GCC) countries like Qatar that enable jihadist individuals and groups to survive and thrive.

Some shariah-adherent nations like Saudi Arabia and the United Arab Emirates (UAE) have already calculated that the jihads their governments, royal families, businesses, and sovereign wealth-funded investments have been underwriting and otherwise supporting now pose a threat to their ruling families. Self-interest and the need for self-preservation have prompted both countries, as well as the Arab League, for example, to declare the Muslim Brotherhood a terrorist organization. The UAE has gone so far as to identify two Brotherhood front groups in the United States – the Council on American Islamic Relations (CAIR) and the Muslim American Society (MAS) as terrorist organizations.[111] Others, like Qatar, though, still use vast sovereign wealth funds and other means to fund jihad, including financial jihad. Such double-games can no longer be tolerated.[112]

- Ending the Western practice of providing undisciplined, discretionary cash to shariah-linked entities (e.g., sovereign sponsors, wealth funds, banks, companies, bond and equity offerings etc.) that currently can attract large-scale financing without any underlying projects or trade transactions. For example, shariah-associated entities have benefited enormously from so-called "structured commodity finance" transactions (a.k.a. "pre-export finance") of the kind that has been used to make available multi-billion-dollar, front-end cash infusions to bad actors in exchange for future deliveries of oil and other commodities at a discounted price.[113]

The U.S. Treasury Department has proven quite effective in going after the sources of terror funding. But it is constrained by the need to sell U.S. bonds to some of these same actors. It must no longer be considered acceptable to ignore, or otherwise fail to counter, the threats posed by jihadi economic warfare.

- Undermining any caliphate currency system the Islamic State might establish by manipulating its price levels to create severe volatility. Any bank accounts identified as belonging to targeted jihadist enemies should be accessed, hacked and manipulated. Offensive cyber methods like these will carry with them the risk of retaliation, of course, especially given the demonstrated cyber sophistication of some of our jihadist enemies. But, as economic war is being waged against us by them, we must strive to protect our assets while taking down theirs.

Vital American interests and our national security cannot be safeguarded with a mindset that assumes the only threat we face emanates from "violent extremism" and that most cultures, nation states, people and religions incline naturally to peace and tolerance. Unfortunately, these are wishes not accurate reflections of reality.[114]

Arguably, the most dangerous aspect of rooting U.S. policy in such wishful thinking is the willful blindness towards the stealthy subversion of civilization jihad, which includes economic warfare. Only by recognizing this threat in all of its manifestations and by working diligently to strengthen, among other things, our own economic posture and warfare capabilities can the U.S. and the rest of the Free World prevent their submission to shariah that the Global Jihad Movement believes it is called by Allah to achieve.

NEW THEATERS OF OPERATION

There are two important fronts in the present stage of the long-running War for the Free World that were not addressed in President Reagan's prescription for prevailing in the last one, National Security Decision Directive 75. As a practical matter, the first – ideological and other forms of warfare in the cyber domain – simply did not exist in the early 1980s. And while Soviet Communist penetration of and subversion inside the United States had been a persistent problem for decades,[115] Mr. Reagan's strategy did not specifically task the government to counter it. Both of these challenges must be considered to be threats for the purposes of an NSDD 75 2.0 and dealt with effectively.

ENGAGING IN CYBER WARFARE

THE THREAT ENVIRONMENT

In stark contrast to the Cold War era, today even individual hackers – to say nothing of terrorist groups or hostile nations – can and do attack this country through computer-based techniques. To cite one example, such a cyber attack in late 2014 against a U.S.-based entity, Sony Pictures Entertainment, was formally attributed to North Korea by the FBI. Others have noted that North Korea may not have acted alone; China at a minimum likely knew about the attack. The attack underscored not only the vulnerability of private sector proprietary data and employees' personal information.[116] The Sony incident also brought to the fore hard questions about the susceptibility of U.S. government agencies and activities and that of our critical infrastructure to hostile powers' rapidly evolving capabilities for cyber espionage and attack.

Furthermore, despite President Obama's promise of "a proportional response" for the Sony attack,[117] and passing references to "cyber attacks" and "cyber security" in national security documents including the March 2011 Presidential Policy Directive/PPD-8 on National Preparedness[118] and the June 2011 National Security Strategy,[119] it is not at all clear exactly what authorities exist in U.S. law or policy for the Department of Defense or the Intelligence Community to conduct offensive or retaliatory cyber attacks. The 2001 Authorization for the Use of Military Force[120] gives the president the authority to "use all necessary and appropriate force" to protect the country from further attacks, but does not explicitly address cyber operations.

The cyber threat has grown exponentially in the past few years as sophisticated techniques that were not so long ago assessed to be the exclusive domain of national intelligence services have proliferated worldwide among enemies of Western civilization at all levels. Indeed, the cyber threat has become sufficiently acute that top U.S. security officials at the CIA, the FBI, the National Security Agency and the White House are publicly warning about the implications of emerging asymmetric threats posed by the offensive cyber capabilities of an array of adversaries.[121] These range from hostile nation states like China, Iran, and North Korea, to sub-national Islamic terrorists like IS to assorted transnational anarchists, cyber warriors and hackers of all stripes.

Increasingly, we confront not only the increasing sophistication of such attackers at all levels, but in the objectives of the cyber weaponeers. Heretofore, cyber operations against governments typically focused on stealing military and state secrets. Those against firms – including, notably, defense contractors –

sought proprietary information for economic advantage. And those against individuals were mostly about identity theft and credit card fraud.

Today's cyber attacks today are often politically/ideologically motivated. Agenda-driven cyber warfare of the 21st Century seeks not only to inflict catastrophic damage against national critical infrastructure but to conduct jihad, wage psychological warfare against enemy populations and suppress free speech and expression.

The Nature of Cyber Warfare Today

Examples of this new object of cyberwarfare include the following:

In February 2014, a massive cyber attack hit the Las Vegas Sands Casino, owned by Sheldon Adelson, who a few months earlier, had made public comments about confronting a belligerently nuclearizing Iran.[122] The apparent Iranian response marked the first time a jihadist regime had sought to destroy an American corporate entity in retribution against an individual U.S. citizen.

Then, in December 2014, a stunning report entitled *Operation Cleaver* was released by a private U.S. cyber forensic firm, Cylance.[123] It revealed that a network of Iranian hackers has, since 2012, "directly attacked, established persistence in and extracted highly sensitive materials from the networks of government agencies and major critical infrastructure companies in the following countries: Canada, China, England, France, Germany, India, Israel, Kuwait, Mexico, Pakistan, Qatar, Saudi Arabia, South Korea, Turkey, United Arab Emirates, and the United States."

Ominously, the Iranian network, which is still in operation, has managed successfully to infiltrate and obtain the ability to attack from the inside a range of critical infrastructure around the world, including: oil, gas, energy, public utilities, transportation, hospitals, telecommunications technology, education, aerospace and defense contractors, chemical companies, and government agencies. The FBI took the threat seriously enough to issue a warning to U.S. defense and energy firms, advising them to take steps to protect their networks from hackers.[124]

As noted above, Sony Pictures sustained a highly publicized cyber attack that destroyed computer hard drives and stole large quantities of commercial and personal data. The FBI concluded that the North Korean government was responsible, likely in an attempt to preclude the release of a film that spoofed a CIA assassination operation against North Korean leader, Kim Jong-Un.[125] Once again, a hostile nation state evidently deployed state cyber assets to target a private sector entity, this time in a pre-emptive bid to shut down free expression.

As we have seen, in light of the highly public nature of this attack, President

Obama evidently felt compelled publicly to declare that the United States would respond in a "proportional" manner. And when North Korea's already limited links to the Internet went completely down on 22 December 2014 after several days of instability, few doubted that someone had struck back.[126]

Recognizing, however, that a line had been crossed in the battle spaces of international cyber warfare, Rep. Patrick Meehan, chairman of the House Committee on Homeland Security's Subcommittee on Cybersecurity on 18 December 2014 warned of the "growing danger of the cyber threat" that could at some point hit the U.S. electric grid.[127] Both of the cyber attacks against the Sands Casino and Sony were attributed to nation states that targeted the free speech of American citizens, but unless urgent measures are taken to secure the presently unhardened U.S. civilian electric grid, a great deal more than casinos and movies is at risk.

Actual physical damage of a very high magnitude caused by cyber attack must now be a real concern. As demonstrated in the Cylance report, for instance, the extensive, highly sophisticated cyber capabilities of the Iranian regime already are a reality, while North Korea (which has worked closely with Iran on its nuclear weapons and ballistic missile programs for years) clearly aims for cyber weaponeer status, too. A report published in mid-December 2014 by the German Federal Office for Information Security shows the level of physical destruction that can be accomplished by skilled hackers.[128] According to the report, a German steel factory suffered massive damage after hackers gained access to the controls of a blast furnace. There was no indication in public reports about who might have been responsible.

If anything, these threats are certain to grow in frequency and intensity in the future. National Public Radio reported on December 26, 2014:

There are global underground markets where anyone can buy and sell all the malicious code for an attack like the one North Korea is accused of unleashing on Sony Pictures. These underground markets not only make it more difficult to trace who is responsible for any given hack — they also make launching a sophisticated attack against a global company much easier. In a sense, these brokers are the arms dealers of the digital age. They act as go-betweens – connecting researchers and hackers with buyers, governments and organizations searching for back doors into computer networks.[129]

Global Jihadis Take Aim at Western Audiences

Given the state of the art, the proliferation of relevant skill sets and the potential for devastating attacks, the acquisition of nation state-level cyber capabilities by sub-national and transnational jihadist entities likely was inevitable.

But the exploitation of a Western-developed medium like the Internet, which has revolutionized human ability to access and share information both individually and collaboratively, for the purpose of destroying that civilization, is acutely ironic.

Jihadist groups like al Qaeda first began to use online chat rooms, forums and websites in the 1980s. But today's jihadis – notably, those associated with the Islamic State – are light years beyond those early cyber pioneers. Technologically adept, often university educated at American and European universities, IS cyber weaponeers have made the Internet their playground, conducting communications, offensive attack operations, proselytizing, propaganda, psychological operations, recruitment, and training, all in cyberspace.

The development of an array of mobile devices coupled with the emergence of social media as the dominant medium of communication enables an overwhelmingly young generation of jihadis to adapt instantaneously to new apps, latching onto Facebook, Flickr, Instagram, Twitter, YouTube and every other channel that allows them to project their messages, attract tech-savvy Muslim youth around the world to their cause, raise funds, hijack drones and aircraft, train members in cyber security and wreak havoc with hacking attacks against financial institutions, critical infrastructure, and individuals alike.

The laptop, the smartphone, and the tablet are as indispensable to 21st Century jihad as the AK-47 – and in fact, feature prominently alongside them in IS online imagery.[130]

Jihadist advances in cyber warfare have become impossible to ignore particularly since the 2011 outbreak of the Syrian rebellion. The young fighters who flock by the tens of thousands to IS' black flag of jihad bring with them cyber skill sets on a par with those of any of the younger generation in the West. Indeed, many hundreds of them were born and raised in places like Australia, Canada, Europe and the United States. Using the range of technical platforms – laptops, notebooks, and smart phones – these cyber warriors are globally connected and know how to make sure their content is viewable anytime, anywhere.

And it is that content that has both horrified and mesmerized a global audience. Professional quality psy-op videos of the most heinous human rights abuses, including amputations, beheadings, crucifixions, prisoner executions, and sex slavery are carefully calibrated at once to appeal to potential Muslim recruits and to terrify their non-Muslim enemies (all while justifying their barbarity with meticulous citations from the Islamic canon). Yet another objective, as detailed in the slickly-produced, full-color online IS magazine, *Dabiq*,[131] is to prod emotionally-driven Western societies to send ground troops to engage in the final battles of Armageddon that the jihadist eschatology demands in order to usher in the final Day of Judgment. This generation of jihadis demonstrates technical skills that are rivaled only by their mastery of psychological warfare against Western society – even as our national security leadership persists in describing them as "unimaginative" misguided thugs "bereft of ideas."

Threat Convergence: A 'Red-Green Axis' in Cyberspace

Global cyber interconnectivity also allows like-minded enemies of the U.S. and Western civilization more generally to join forces in cyberspace. The so-called "Red-Green Axis" unites anarchists, communists, leftists, and assorted revolutionaries with Islamic jihadis in an unlikely cause whose only point of ideological commonality is a shared hatred of Judeo-Christian-based liberal Western civilization. Both the leftists and the jihadis seek to overthrow the current world order and impose in its place a new one characterized primarily by totalitarianism. Both likewise have proven all-too-willing to resort to ruthless carnage in their quest to destroy the existing system.

The interfaith dialogue movement is one such nexus of the 'reds' and the 'greens.' In the U.S., jihadist front groups for the Muslim Brotherhood engage aggressively through the platforms of the online social media with gullible faith communities (both Christian and Jewish) and their equally clueless leadership, which often are distinctly progressive in outlook. Online message boards, publications, and websites promote a rosy image of Islamic doctrine, history, law, and scriptures and serve as portals to critical-thinking-free ecumenical interaction. Little do most of these religious communities realize that the founder of the interfaith dialogue movement was none other than the radical leftist and avowed atheist, Saul Alinsky.[132]

The anti-Israel Boycott-Divest-Sanction (BDS) movement likewise joins leftist, often religiously-affiliated, individuals and groups to virulently antisemitic jihadist organizations like American Muslims for Palestine and Students for Justice in Palestine. University campuses across the U.S. serve as incubators for such activities, much of it advanced across the most natural medium for the country's tech-savvy younger generation, the Internet.[133]

Cyberspace also facilitates the co-option by jihadist forces of traditional leftist causes and vocabulary. Long the favored arena of progressives, outreach to minority and underprivileged communities now is being adopted in a calculated campaign by the U.S. Muslim Brotherhood, which slyly embeds its jihadist objectives in the images and jargon of social justice and human rights. The very lexicon of oppression and victimhood used to great effect not only by the legitimate civil rights movement, but the far more radical Black Panthers and

Symbionese Liberation Army, is in the process of being rebranded for use by the pro-jihad and shariah forces at work in America.

Street rioters in Ferguson, Missouri who erupted in violence following the August 2014 shooting of a young black criminal by the white police officer he had assaulted, for example, were actively targeted by the Islamic State in a coordinated online campaign to make common cause against U.S. legal authorities. Facebook and Twitter were used aggressively by IS jihadis to encourage more violence from the Ferguson rioters with graphic imagery of IS fighters pledging "Hey blacks, ISIS will save you" and photos of Malcom X.[134] Protests were coordinated nationwide by front groups of the Workers World Party, a small New York-based Marxist-Leninist group that is openly supportive of, and reportedly funded by, the government of North Korea.[135]

Last, but not least, the U.S. Council of Muslim Organizations (USCMO), the first Muslim Brotherhood political party in the United States (established in 2014) likewise has adopted a calculated strategy designed to project especially to the African American population its focus on diversity and race relations.[136] Solidarity with anti-Israel and pro-HAMAS street demonstrators gives the USCMO another opportunity to insert itself into the political milieu of the red-green axis. During a July 22, 2014 event in downtown Chicago, IL, USCMO members joined in protests against the then-ongoing Israeli Defense Forces (IDF) Operation Protective Edge in the Gaza Strip. Once again, Facebook and Twitter served as the cyber battle space for a swarm of leftist and Muslim HAMAS supporters.[137]

FIGHTING BACK: A COUNTER-CYBER JIHAD STRATEGY

Counterterrorism and national security officials would seem to be acutely aware of the cyber jihad threat, having issued multiple reports and warnings about the proliferation of jihadist activities in cyberspace at least since shortly after the 9/11 attacks. Thus far, though, the jihadis are winning in the cyber battlespace. Western government attempts to shut down terrorist websites and social media accounts amount to little more than a "whack-a-mole" shell game, as the cyber-savvy jihadis open new ones faster than the authorities can counter them. The White House and Congress must demonstrate commitment and leadership in the fight against cyber jihad.

The National Security Agency and U.S. Cyber Command have the lead but have yet to fully develop their doctrine, both defensive and offensive, for operating in cyber space. Integration of an offensive cyberwarfare mentality is critical to establishing deterrence against enemies all-too-ready to deploy devastating cyber-attacks against civilian targets as well as military ones.

U.S. laws have not kept pace either with the rapid development of digital combat. As the former head of the U.S. Cyber Command (as well as former Director of the National Security Agency), Lt. Gen. Keith B. Alexander, prepared for his confirmation hearing in 2010, he wrote to members of the Senate Armed Services Committee that cyber warfare was evolving so quickly that there was a "mismatch between our technical capabilities to conduct operations and the governing laws and policies."[138]

Yet to be delineated, for instance, is the role of the military's Cyber Command on U.S. soil – where traditionally the military may only operate on direct orders of the president – and yet, given the borderless nature of cyber warfare, a battlespace where enemy attacks already occur on a regular basis. Further, the ongoing debate between the Department of Defense, which sees cyber operations falling within the purview of traditional military activity under the laws of armed conflict as governed by Title 10 of the U.S. Code, and the Intelligence Community, which contends that cyber operations by nature are inherently covert and therefore should fall under the provisions of Title 50 has yet to be resolved.[139]

To do so will require in this domain, as with the rest of the battlespace of the War for the Free World, an acknowledgement that there is a Global Jihad Movement in operation against us and that it possesses a guiding ideology that can be studied and known: shariah. Here, once again, U.S. national security leadership – from the Commander-in-Chief to the Intelligence Community to the Pentagon and Homeland Security Department to the halls of Congress – must abandon the willful blindness in which it has indulged for at least the past thirteen years. And it must develop and execute an effective counter-jihad strategy that integrates cyber warfare capabilities at least as sophisticated as those the enemy is using against us.

Given that the heart of the global social media network lies within U.S.-based high tech firms, their cooperation in blocking the ability of cyber jihadists to conduct operations over the Internet is crucial. A series of national security briefings for the leaders of such social media hosts as Facebook, Google, Microsoft and Twitter at least would ensure they could not claim ignorance about the problem.

The White House should convene a Blue Ribbon panel of U.S. technology leadership to formulate strategies for confronting the threat in coordination with federal agencies. Congressional hearings that compel testimony from corporations that host al Qaeda, Islamic State and other jihadist websites about the steps they are taking – or are failing to take – to curtail jihadi cyber activity likewise would be beneficial.

Certainly there are additional steps that must be taken in this realm, but the foundation of a counter-cyber jihad strategy must rest on a counter jihad mindset, appropriate legal authorities and policy directives, and harnessing the cooperative expertise of government and the private sector.

DEFEATING CIVILIZATION JIHAD ON THE HOME FRONT

The *Explanatory Memorandum on the General Strategic Goal of the Group in North America* is the secret plan of the Muslim Brotherhood to "destroy Western civilization from within." The Justice Department introduced it into evidence in the largest terrorism financing trial in U.S. history – the Holy Land Foundation trial in Richardson, Texas in 2007-2008. The defendants did not contest the authenticity of the document.

As this document makes clear, what the Brotherhood has done since the founding of the Muslim Students Association in 1962 is systematically to build an infrastructure of front groups, mosques, Islamic societies and other entities to conduct what it calls "civilization jihad" against the United States. The *Explanatory Memorandum* identified twenty-nine of them in an addendum entitled "Our Organizations and Organizations of our Friends." The number of such fronts and like-minded entities has increased exponentially since that document was written in 1991.[140]

Among the focuses of the civilization jihadists' penetration and subversion operations are the following:

- Keeping the "infidels" ignorant of the true nature and progress of efforts to insinuate shariah into Western societies. As described elsewhere, the application of what amounts to shariah blasphemy and slander restrictions to what government leaders, security personnel and average citizens can know and work to counter is an enormous force multiplier for the stealthy jihad.

- Demanding and securing accommodations for shariah-adherent Muslims and other concessions. This is a key part of establishing both symbolically and in more tangible ways the practice of submission to Islamic supremacism.

- Utilizing educational vehicles to promote the cause of Islamic supremacism. Civilization jihadists have made significant inroads into American academia by dint of the "red-green axis" with U.S. "progressives" who dominate our educational system. State-approved textbooks, teaching plans and Common Core-directed core-curricula are vehicles for extolling Islam while deprecating Christianity, Judaism and other faiths and for promoting submission to the former.

Turkish jihadist Fethullah Gulen has established over 140 taxpayer-financed charter schools for this purpose across America. His movement must rank as one of the most effective influence operation in state-level politics in the last century. In his words: "You must move in the arteries of the system without anyone noticing your existence until you reach all the power centers... until the conditions are ripe, they [the followers] must continue like this. If they do something prematurely, the world will crush our heads, and Muslims will suffer everywhere..."[141]

- "Bridge-building" and interfaith "dialogue." The stealth jihadists have made enormous inroads in the faith community by enlisting non-Muslim clerics to argue on First Amendment grounds against opposition to shariah. This practice provides protection to and enables the civilization jihad.

- Promoting Shariah-Compliant Finance. As noted above, this industry is generally portrayed in Western capital markets as an innocent vehicle for repatriating petro-dollars. In practice, it is an instrument of jihad, aimed at coopting influential capitalists and gaining access to and influence over their financial affairs and political allies.

- Insinuating shariah into U.S. courts. In Britain, civilization jihadists have secured the establishment of 87 shariah courts that operate side-by-side with English Common Law courts. In the United States, the Muslim Brotherhood has established shariah arbitration facilities within the chapters of their largest front group, the Islamic Society of North America. They have also sought to have shariah, rather than American laws adopted pursuant to the U.S. Constitution and state public policy, be used to adjudicate cases in state and federal courts. A recent study found 143 examples of such efforts in 35 states.[142]

- Placing Muslim Brothers into positions from which they can exercise influence. Gaining access to government agencies and elected officials has long been a priority for civilization jihadists. They have succeeded in administrations of both parties.[143] And the resulting influence operations have operated synergistically with and contributed significantly to the inroads made in many of the preceding focuses for the stealth jihad.

COUNTERING THE CIVILIZATION JIHAD AT HOME

The skill of the Muslim Brotherhood and others, like the Organization of Islamic Cooperation, engaged in civilization jihad in the West has made the job of challenging and neutralizing such stealthy subversion considerably more difficult. Portraying those who warn of their agenda and activities as racists, bigots and Islamophobes has enabled these shariah-adherent groups and their spokesmen to suppress critics and spook politicians.

If we are to prevail over those who seek to force us to submit to shariah, however, it is not enough to do neutralize the wellsprings of this totalitarian ideology and its followers abroad. We must also counter shariah and the jihadists here at home.

The following are illustrative examples of initiatives that would advance those necessary goals:

- Muslims who reject shariah's seditious agenda and oppose its imposition on others should be promoted and empowered. The practice must end whereby federal and state-level government agencies of "engagement" with or "outreach" to those who purport to be "leaders" of the Muslim American community but typically are, in fact, simply shariah- adherent Islamic supremacists associated with the Muslim Brotherhood.

- In April 2012, five U.S. lawmakers – Representatives Michele Bachmann, Louie Gohmert, Trent Franks, Lynn Westmoreland and Tom Rooney – wrote the Inspectors General of five federal agencies (the Departments of State, Justice, Defense, Homeland Security and the Office of the Director of National Security). They sought investigations of individuals who were either employees of or advisors to those agencies and who have been shown to have ties to or sympathies with the Muslim Brotherhood. The object was to establish whether such individuals were having an influence on U.S. policies that were increasingly aligning with the dictates of the Brotherhood.[144]

  While these legislators were subsequently excoriated for even raising the question,[145] the need for an answer is as great as ever. Congressional hearings should be held for that purpose.

- In the 113th Congress, Rep. Bachmann introduced legislation to designate the Muslim Brotherhood as a terrorist organization.[146] This legislation should be reintroduced, enacted and used as a basis for rolling up and shutting down its front groups in the United States.

- In 2011, a peer-reviewed study by Mordechai Kedar and David Yerushalmi appeared first in the *Middle East Quarterly* under the title "Shariah and Violence in American Mosques."[147] It described the results of an undercover investigation of 100 randomly selected representative American mosques aimed at measuring the correlation between shariah adherence and dogma calling for violence against non-believers. Over eighty percent presented evidence of both adherence to shariah and an advocacy of violent jihad. Such mosques are not engaged in the protected practice of religion. They are incubators of, at best, subversion and, at worst, violence and should be treated accordingly.

- The United States must terminate the practice of issuing visas for shariah-adherent imams who often seek to use such mosques for purposes antithetical to tolerant religious practice and to the Constitution.

- Similarly, the federal government must stop using refugee resettlement programs, political asylum, visa lotteries, amnesties, etc. to bring large numbers of shariah-adherent Muslims to this country. All too often, they: have no real prospect of assimilation or loyalty to the United States; congregate in what amount to shariah-enclaves; and, in some cases, once credentialed to live here, engage in acts of jihad overseas – and possibly plan to return to engage in them here.

- The U.S. must revoke the citizenship of naturalized Americans who, in seeking to insinuate shariah-compliant norms into civil society, have violated their oath of naturalization and allegiance to defend the Constitution of the United States.

- American academic institutions that accept funds from shariah-adherent individuals or governments must be required to disclose fully the extent of those payments and the purpose for which they are provided. Where that purpose amounts to promoting shariah or civilization jihadist agendas (e.g., interfaith dialogue, "Muslim-Christian understanding," etc.), the institution should be discouraged from hosting such activities. At the very least, they should be required to offer corresponding educational activities exposing the true nature of shariah and the Muslim Brotherhood's operations, although the legal enforcement of such measures likely will require new legislation that identifies and bans Brotherhood operations as hostile or subversive to the U.S. legal order.

  Legal enforcement of such measures likely will require new legislation that identifies and bans Brotherhood operations as hostile or subversive to the U.S. legal order. Until then, taxpayer funding of such institutions should be banned and their 501(c)(3) status revoked, or, at a minimum, conditions for such funding and tax status should be reserved for those institutions not promoting shariah in any way.

- Firms engaging in Shariah-Compliant Finance must be required to disclose the nature of shariah, the names and roles of shariah advisors involved in investment decisions and the expectation that some of the proceeds may be used to support jihad.

CONCLUSION

The United States has confronted in the past totalitarian ideologies determined to secure global hegemony and our destruction. Time and time again, we have come together as a nation to counter and defeat Nazism, Fascism, Japanese imperialism and Soviet communism.

Today's ideological threat is the more dangerous for its masquerading as a religion, its global footprint and the fact that its adherents have, in myriad ways, successfully penetrated our government and civil society institutions. The success of shariah's civilization jihadists, in particular, has contributed materially to the diminishing of our defenses against this threat and intensified the peril we face as a free people, society and world.

While the hour is late and the odds are getting longer by the day, we have it within us as Americans once again to muster the resolve and the resources to: understand this enemy; adopt a proven strategy for countering such ideologically driven foes; and put the country on the war footing needed to see it through to victory.

The Tiger Team offers this blueprint for such a course of action in the hope that the American people and our elected representatives will take the formal steps needed to articulate and implement such a strategy modeled after President Reagan's National Security Decision Directive 75 – starting with the adoption by the Congress of a Declaration of War/Authorization of the Use of Military Force against the Global Jihad Movement and the ideology that makes it so dangerous, shariah.

DRAFT CONGRESSIONAL DECLARATION OF WAR AGAINST THE GLOBAL JIHAD MOVEMENT

XXXX, 2015

JOINT RESOLUTION Declaring that a state of war exists between the Global Jihad Movement and the Government and the people of the United States and making provisions to prosecute the same.

Whereas the Global Jihad Movement consists of nations, organizations and movements that seek to wage, or materially enable jihad (warfare) against non-Muslims as well as those Muslims deemed insufficiently adherent to the Islamic faith, for the purpose of imposing a global political order governed by the doctrine of shariah, and administered by a ruling political entity called a caliphate;

Whereas the Global Jihad Movement consists of entities that carry out violent jihad as well as those that seek, through non- or pre-violent means, materially to enable the success of the jihadists by undermining the ability of the United States to challenge and/or counter effectively the triumph of shariah;

Whereas entities waging or materially enabling jihad against the United States and its national security interests include, but are not limited to, the Islamic State in Iraq and al-Sham (ISIS); al-Qa'eda; Hamas; Hizballah; the Islamic Republic of Iran; the Taliban; Boko Haram; al-Shabaab; Ansar al-Shariah; the Muslim Brotherhood; and the Organization of Islamic Cooperation (OIC);

Whereas the ideology of jihad poses a threat to the security and sovereignty of the United States, and therefore requires a comprehensive response from the United States Government in the military, intelligence, law enforcement, political, financial, and informational spheres akin to that authorized by President Ronald Reagan's National Security Decision Directive 75 with respect to Soviet Communism;

Whereas the embrace by Islamic authorities globally of jihad notwithstanding, millions of Muslims worldwide – including within the United States – seek neither to wage nor materially enable violent jihad, nor wish to have shariah imposed on their communities or others:

Therefore be it Resolved by the Senate and House of Representatives of the United States of America in Congress assembled,

That the state of war between the United States and the Global Jihad Movement which has thus been thrust upon the United States is hereby formally declared;

and the President is hereby authorized and directed to employ the entire armed forces of the United States and the resources of the Government to carry on war against the Global Jihad Movement; and, to bring the conflict to a successful termination, all of the resources of the country are hereby pledged by the Congress of the United States.

DRAFT AUTHORIZATION OF THE USE OF MILITARY FORCE AND OTHER MEANS AGAINST THE GLOBAL JIHAD MOVEMENT

JOINT RESOLUTION

To authorize the use of United States Armed Forces, and other resources of the Government of the United States, against the Global Jihad Movement.

Whereas the Global Jihad Movement consists of nations and organizations that seek to wage, or materially enable, *jihad* (warfare) against non-Muslims as well as those Muslims deemed insufficiently adherent to the Islamic faith, for the purpose of imposing a global order governed by the doctrine of shariah, and administered by a caliphate;

Whereas the Global Jihad Movement consists of entities that carry out violent jihad as well as those that seek, through non- or pre-violent means, materially to enable the success of the Jihads by undermining the ability of the United States to counter effectively the triumph of shariah;

Whereas entities waging violent jihad against the United States and its national security interests include, but are not limited to, the Islamic State in Iraq and al-Sham (ISIS); al-Qa'eda; Hamas; Hizballah; the Islamic Republic of Iran; the Taliban; Boko Haram; al-Shabaab; Ansar al-Shariah.

Whereas entities materially enabling jihad against the United States and its national security interests include, but are not limited to, the Muslim Brotherhood; and the Organization of Islamic Cooperation (OIC);

Whereas the ideology of jihad poses a threat to the security and sovereignty of the United States, pledges the overthrow of the Constitution of the United States and therefore requires a comprehensive response from the United States Government in the military, intelligence, law enforcement, political, financial, and informational spheres akin to that authorized by President Ronald Reagan's National Security Decision Directive 75 with respect to Soviet Communism;

Whereas the embrace by Islamic authorities globally of jihad notwithstanding, millions of Muslims worldwide – including within the United States – seek neither to wage nor materially to enable violent or non- or pre-violent jihad, nor wish to have shariah imposed on their communities or others;

Resolved by the Senate and House of Representatives of the United States of America in Congress assembled,

SECTION 1. SHORT TITLE.

This joint resolution may be cited as the "Authorization for the Use of Military Force Against the Global Jihad Movement of 2015."

SEC. 2. AUTHORIZATION FOR USE OF UNITED STATES ARMED FORCES

a. IN GENERAL – The President is authorized to use all necessary and appropriate force against those nations and organizations waging **violent** jihad against the United States or in contravention to the national security of the United States.

The President is authorized to use all necessary and appropriate military assets except deadly force against those nations and organizations waging **non-violent or materially enabling violent** jihad against the United States or in contravention to the national security of the United States.

b. WAR POWERS RESOLUTION REQUIREMENTS

1. SPECIFIC STATUTORY AUTHORIZATION. – Consistent with section 8(a)(1) of the War Powers Resolution, Congress declares that this section is intended to constitute specific statutory authorization within the meaning of section 5(b) of the War Powers Resolution.

2. APPLICABILITY OF OTHER REQUIREMENTS. – Nothing in this Act supersedes any requirement of the War Powers Resolution.

SEC. 3. SUPPORT FOR UNITED STATES HOMELAND SECURITY, LAW ENFORCEMENT, FINANCIAL, AND INFORMATIONAL EFFORTS

The Congress of the United States supports the use of federal homeland security, law enforcement, financial, and informational mechanisms against the Global Jihad Movement to—

1. Fully secure all land and maritime borders and ports of entry against illegal entry into the United States by individuals, or agents of organizations or foreign nations, seeking to carry out Jihad attacks or engage in material support for Jihad activities;

2. Undertake law enforcement operations within or at the borders of the United States in order to identify and prevent acts of jihad or material support for Jihad activities;

3. Deny Jihad entities financial revenue, including through the maximum deployment of domestic energy resources and the denial of access to global financial markets;

4. Secure information dominance over the Global Jihad Movement through the use of information warfare to undermine the movement and its objectives.

SEC. 4. AUTHORIZATION OF MILITARY CUSTODY FOR INTELLIGENCE-GATHERING PURPOSES

The Congress of the United States authorizes that individuals waging or materially enabling jihad on behalf of, or at the instigation of, a Jihad government or entity, who are captured by the United States military abroad, or by federal law enforcement within or at the borders of the United States, shall be detained initially by the United States armed forces for the purpose of gathering intelligence before any transfer to civilian authorities, and, in the case of foreign nationals, detention until trial by military commission in Guantanamo Bay.

APPENDIX

NATIONAL SECURITY DECISION DIRECTIVE 75

Approved For Release 2008/02/20:CIA-RDP97M00248R000401070001-8

THE WHITE HOUSE | WASHINGTON | January 17, 1983

National Security Decision Directive Number 75

U.S. RELATIONS WITH THE USSR

U.S. policy toward the Soviet Union will consist of three elements: eternal resistance to Soviet imperialism; internal pressure on the USSR to weaken the sources of Soviet imperialism; and negotiations to eliminate, on the basis of strict reciprocity, outstanding disagreements. Specifically, U.S. tasks are:

1. To contain and over time reverse Soviet expansionism by competing effectively on a sustained basis with the Soviet Union in all international arenas – particularly in the overall military balance and in geographical regions of propriety concern to the United States. This will remain the primary focus of U.S. policy toward the USSR.

2. To promote, within the narrow limits available to us, the process of change in the Soviet Union toward a more pluralistic political and economic system in which the power of the privileged ruling elite is gradually reduced. The U.S. recognizes that Soviet aggressiveness has deep roots in the internal system, and that relations with the USSR should therefore take into account whether or not they help to strengthen this system and its capacity to engage in aggression.

3. To engage the Soviet Union in negotiations to attempt to reach agreements which protect and enhance U.S. interests and which are consistent with the principle of strict reciprocity and mutual interest. This is important when the Soviet Union is in the midst of a process of political succession.

In order to implement this threefold strategy, the U.S. must convey clearly to Moscow that unacceptable behavior will incur costs that would outweigh any gains. At the same time, the U.S. must make clear to the Soviets that genuine restraint in their behavior would create the possibility of an East-West relationship that might bring important benefits for the Soviet Union. It is particularly important that this message be conveyed clearly during the succession period, since this may be a particularly opportune time for external forces to affect the policies of Brezhnev's successors.

Shaping the Soviet Environment: Arenas of Engagement

Implementation of the U.S. policy must focus on shaping the environment in which Soviet decisions are made both in a wide variety of functional and geopolitical arenas and in the U.S.-Soviet bilateral relationship.

A. Functional

1. Military Strategy: The U.S. must modernize its military forces – both nuclear and conventional – so that Soviet leaders perceive that the U.S. is determined never to accept a second place or a deteriorating military posture. Soviet calculations of possible war outcomes under any contingency must always result in outcomes so unfavorable to the USSR that there would be no incentive for the Soviet leaders to initiate an attack. The future strength of U.S. military capabilities must be assured. U.S. military technology advances must be exploited, while controls over transfer of military related/dual-use technology, products, and services must be tightened.

In Europe, the Soviets must be faced with a reinvigorated NATO. In the Far East we must ensure that the Soviets cannot count on a secure flank in a global war. Worldwide, U.S. general purpose forces must be strong and flexible enough to affect Soviet calculations in a wide variety of contingencies. In the Third World, Moscow must know that areas of interest to the U.S. cannot be attacked or threatened without risk of serious U.S. military countermeasures.

2. Economic Policy: U.S. policy on economic relations with the USSR must serve strategic and foreign policy goals as well as economic interests. In this context, U.S. objectives are:

- Above all, to ensure that East-West economic relations do not facilitate the Soviet military buildup. This requires prevention of the transfer of technology and equipment that would make a substantial contribution directly or indirectly to Soviet military power.

- To avoid subsidizing the Soviet economy or unduly easing the burden of Soviet resources allocation decisions, so as not to dilute pressures for structural change in the Soviet system.

- To seek to minimize the potential for Soviet exercise of reverse leverage on Western countries based on trade, energy supply, and financial relationships.

- To permit mutual beneficial trade – without Western subsidization or the creation of Western dependence – with the USSR in non-strategic areas, such as grains.

The U.S. must exercise strong leadership with its Allies and others to develop a common understanding of the strategic implications of East-West trade, building upon the agreement announced November 13, 1982 (see NSDD 66). This approach should involve efforts to reach agreements with the Allies on specific measures, such as: (a) no incremental deliveries of Soviet gas beyond the amounts contracted for from the first stand of the Siberian pipeline; (b) the addition of critical technologies and equipment to the COCOM list, the harmonization of national licensing coordination and effectiveness of international enforcement efforts; (c) controls on advanced technology and equipment beyond the expanded COCOM list, including equipment in the oil and gas sector; (d) further restraints on officially-backed credits such as higher down payments, shortened maturities and an established framework to monitor this process; and (e) the strengthening of the role of the OECD and NATO in East-West trade analysis and policy.

In the longer term, if Soviet behavior should worsen, e.g. an invasion of Poland, we would need to consider extreme measures. Should Soviet behavior improve, carefully calibrated positive economic signals, including a broadening of government-to-government economic contacts, could be considered as a means of demonstrating to the Soviets the benefits that real restraint in their conduct might bring. Such steps could not, however, alter the basic direction of U.S. policy.

3. Political Action: U.S. policy must have an ideological thrust which clearly affirms the superiority of U.S. and Western values of individual dignity and freedom, a free press, free trade unions, free enterprise, and political democracy over the repressive features of Soviet Communism. We need to review and significantly strengthen U.S. instruments of political action including: (a) The President's London initiative to support democratic forces; (b) USG efforts to highlight Soviet human rights violations; and (c) U.S. radio broadcasting policy. The U.S. should:

- Expose at all available fora the double standards employed by the Soviet Union in dealing with difficulties within its own domain and the outside ("capitalist") world (e.g., treatment of labor, policies toward ethnic minorities, use of chemical weapons, etc.)

- Prevent the Soviet propaganda machine from seizing the semantic high-ground in the battle of ideas through the appropriation of such terms as "peace."

B. Geopolitical

1. The Industrial Democracies: An effective response to the Soviet challenge requires close partnership among the industrial democracies, including stronger and more effective collective defense arrangements. The U.S. must provide strong leadership and conduct effective consultations to build consensus and cushion the impact of intra-alliance disagreements. While Allied support of U.S. overall strategy is essential, the U.S. may on occasion be forced to act to protect vital interests without Allied support and even in the face of Allied opposition; even in this event, however, U.S. should consult to the maximum extent possible with its Allies.

2. The Third World: The U.S. must rebuild the credibility of its commitment to resist Soviet encroachment on U.S. interests and those of its allies and friends, and to support effectively those Third World states that are willing to resist Soviet pressures or oppose Soviet initiatives hostile to the United States, or are special targets of Soviet policy. The U.S. effort in the Third World must involve an important role for security assistance and foreign military sales, as well as readiness to use U.S. military forces where necessary to protect vital interests and support endangered Allies and friends. U.S. policy must also involve diplomatic initiatives to promote resolution of regional crises vulnerable to Soviet exploitation, and an appropriate mixture of economic assistance programs and private sector initiatives for Third World countries.

3. The Soviet Empire: There are a number of important weaknesses and vulnerabilities within the Soviet empire which the U.S. should exploit. U.S. policies should seek wherever possible to encourage Soviet allies to distance themselves from Moscow in foreign policy and to move toward democratizations domestically.

(a) Eastern Europe: The primary U.S. objective in Eastern Europe is to loosen Moscow's hold on the region while promoting the cause of human rights in individual East European countries. The U.S. can advance this objective by carefully discriminating in favor of countries that show relative independence from the USSR in their foreign policy, or show a greater degree of internal liberalization. U.S. policies must also make clear that East European countries which reverse movements of liberalization, or drift away from an independent stance in foreign policy, will incur significant costs in their relations with the U.S.

(b) Afghanistan: The U.S. objective is to keep maximum pressure on Moscow for withdrawal and to ensure that the Soviets' political, military, and other costs remain high while the occupation continues.

(c) Cuba: The U.S. must take strong countermeasures to affect the political/military impact of Soviet arms deliveries to Cuba. The U.S. must also provide economic and military assistance to states in Central America and the Caribbean Basin threatened by Cuban destabilizing activities. Finally, the U.S. will seek to reduce the Cuban presence and influence in southern Africa by energetic leadership of the diplomatic effort to achieve a Cuban withdrawal from Angola, or failing that, by increasing the costs of Cuba's role in southern Africa.

(d) Soviet Third World Alliances: U.S. policy will seek to limit and destabilizing activities of Soviet Third World allies and clients. It is a further objective to weaken and, where possible, undermine the existing links between them and the Soviet Union. U.S. policy will include active efforts to encourage democratic movements and forces to bring about political change inside these countries.

4. China: China continues to support U.S. efforts to strengthen the world's defenses against Soviet expansionism. The U.S. should over time seek to achieve enhanced strategic cooperation and policy coordination with China, and to reduce the possibility of a Sino-Soviet rapprochement. The U.S. will continue to pursue a policy of substantially literalized technology transfer and sale of military equipment to China on a case-by-case basis within the parameters of the policy approved by the President in 1981, and defined further in 1982.

5. Yugoslavia: It is U.S policy to support the independence, territorial integrity and national unity of Yugoslavia. Yugoslavia's current difficulties in paying its foreign debts have increased its vulnerability to Soviet pressures. The Yugoslav government, well aware of this vulnerability, would like to reduce its trade dependence on the Soviet Union. It is in our interest to prevent any deterioration in Yugoslavia's economic situation that might weaken its resolve to withstand Soviet pressure.

C. Bilateral Relationships

1. Arms Control: The U.S. will enter into arms control negotiations when they serve U.S. national security objectives. At the same time, U.S. policy recognizes that arms control agreements are not an end in themselves but

are, in combination with U.S. and Allied efforts to maintain the military balance, an important means for enhancing national security and global stability. The U.S. ability to reach satisfactory results in arms control negotiations will inevitably be influenced by the international, the overall state of U.S.-Soviet relations, and the difficulties in defining areas of mutual agreement with an adversary which often seeks unilateral gains. U.S. arms control proposals will be consistent with necessary force modernization plans and will seek to achieve balanced, significant, and verifiable reductions to equal levels of comparable armaments.

2. Official Dialogue: The U.S. should insist that Moscow address the full range of U.S. concerns about Soviet internal behavior and human rights violations, and should continue to resist Soviet efforts to return to a U.S.-Soviet agenda focused primarily on arms control. U.S.-Soviet diplomatic contacts on regional issues can serve U.S. interests if they are used to keep pressure on Moscow for responsible behavior. Such contract can also be useful in driving home to Moscow that the costs of irresponsibility are high, and that the U.S. is prepared to work for pragmatic solutions of regional problems if Moscow is willing seriously to address U.S. concerns. At the same time, such contacts must be handled with care to avoid offering the Soviet Union a role in regional questions it would not otherwise secure.

A continuing dialogue with the Soviets at Foreign Minister level facilitates necessary diplomatic communication with the Soviet leadership and helps to maintain Allied understanding and support for U.S. approach to East-West relations. A summit between President Reagan and his Soviet counterpart might promise similarly beneficial results. At the same time, unless it were carefully handled a summit could be seen as registering an improvement in U.S.-Soviet relations without the changes in Soviet behavior which we have insisted upon. It could therefore generate unrealizable expectations and further stimulate unilateral Allied initiatives toward Moscow.

A summit would not necessarily involve signature of major new U.S.-Soviet agreements. Any summit meeting should achieve the maximum possible positive impact with U.S. Allies and the American public, while making clear to both audiences that improvement in Soviet-American relations depends on changes in Soviet conduct. A summit without such changes must not be understood to signal such improvement.

3. U.S.-Soviet Cooperative Exchanges: The role of U.S.-Soviet cultural, educational, scientific and other cooperative exchanges should be seen in light of the U.S. intention to maintain a strong ideological component in relations with Moscow. The U.S. should not further

dismantle the framework of exchanges; indeed those exchanges which could advance the U.S. objective of promoting positive evolutionary change within the Soviet system should be expanded. At the same time, the U.S. will insist on full reciprocity and encourage its Allies to do so as well. This recognizes that unless the U.S. has an effective official framework for handling exchanges, the Soviets will make separate arrangements with private U.S. sponsors, while denying reciprocal access to the Soviet Union. U.S. policy on exchanges must also take into account the necessity to prevent transfer of sensitive U.S. technology to the Soviet Union.

Priorities in the U.S. Approach: Maximizing Restraining Leverage over Soviet Behavior.

The interrelated tasks of containing the reversing Soviet expansion and promoting evolutionary change within the Soviet Union itself cannot be accomplished quickly. The coming 5-10 years will be a period of considerable uncertainty in which the Soviets may test U.S. resolve by continuing the kind of aggressive international behavior which the U.S. finds unacceptable.

The uncertainties will be exacerbated by the fact that the Soviet Union will be engaged in the unpredictable process of political succession to Brezhnev. The U.S. will not seek to adjust its policies to the Soviet internal conflict, but rather try to create incentives (positive and negative) for the new leadership to adopt policies less detrimental to the U.S. interests. The U.S. will remain ready for improved U.S.-Soviet relations if the Soviet Union makes significant changes in policies of concern to it; the burden for any further deterioration in the relations must fall squarely on Moscow. The U.S. must not yield to pressures to "take the first step."

The existing and projected gap between finite U.S. resources and the level of capabilities needed to implement U.S. strategy makes it essential that the U.S.: (1) establish firm priorities for the use of limited U.S. resources where they will have the greatest restraining impact on the Soviet Union; and (2) mobilize the resources of Allies and friends which are willing to join the U.S. in containing the expansion of Soviet power.

Underlying the full range of U.S. and Western policies must be a strong military capable of action across the entire spectrum of potential conflicts and guided by a well conceived political and military strategy. The heart of U.S. military strategy is to deter attack by the USSR and its allies against the U.S., its Allies, or other important countries, and to defeat such an attack should deterrence fail. Although unilateral U.S. efforts must lead the way in rebuilding Western military strength to counter the Soviet threat, the protection of Western interests will require increased U.S. cooperation with Allied and other states and greater utilization of their resources. This military strategy will be combined with a political strategy attaching high priority to the following objectives:

- Sustaining steady, long-term growth in U.S. defense spending and capabilities – both nuclear and conventional. This is the most important way of conveying to the Soviets U.S. resolve and political staying-power.

- Creating a long-term Western consensus for dealing with the Soviet Union. This will require that the U.S. exercise strong leadership in developing policies to deal with the multifaceted Soviet threat to Western interests. It will require that the U.S. take Allied concerns into account, and also that U.S. Allies take into equal account U.S. concerns. In this connection, and in addition to pushing Allies to spend more on defense, the U.S. must make a serious effort to negotiate arms control agreements consistent with U.S. military strategy and necessary force modernization plans, and should seek to achieve balanced, significant and verifiable reductions to equal levels of comparable armaments. The U.S. must also develop, together with Allies, a unified Western approach to East-West economic relations, implementing the agreement announced on November 13, 1982.

- Maintenance of a strategic relationship with China, and efforts to minimize opportunities for a Sino-soviet rapprochement

- Building and sustaining a major ideological/political offensive which, together with other efforts, will be designed to bring about evolutionary change of the Soviet system. This must be a long-term and sophisticated program, given the nature of the Soviet system.

- Effective opposition to Moscow's efforts to consolidate its position in Afghanistan. This will require that the U.S. continue efforts to promote Soviet withdrawal in the context of a negotiated settlement of the conflict. At the same time, the U.S. must keep pressure on Moscow for withdrawal and ensure that Soviet costs on the ground are high

- Blocking the expansion of Soviet influence in the critical Middle East and Southwest Asia regions. This will require both continued efforts to seek a political solution to the Arab-Israeli conflict and to bolster U.S. relations with moderate states in the region, and a sustained U.S. defense commitment to deter Soviet military encroachments.

- Maintenance of international pressure on Moscow to permit a relaxation of the current repression in Poland and a longer-term increase in diversity and independence throughout Eastern Europe. This will require that the

U.S. continue to impose costs on the Soviet Union for its behavior in Poland. It will also require that the U.S. maintain a U.S. policy of differentiation among European countries.

- Neutralization and reduction of the threat to U.S. national security interests posed by the Soviet-Cuban relationship. This will require that the U.S. use a variety of instruments, including diplomatic efforts and U.S. security and economic assistance. The U.S. must also retain the option of using of its military forces to protect vital U.S. security interests against threats which may arise from the Soviet-Cuban connection.

Articulating the U.S. Approach: Sustaining Public and Congressional Support.

The policy outlined above is one for the long haul. It is unlikely to yield a rapid breakthrough in bilateral relations with the Soviet Union. In the absence of dramatic near-term victories in the U.S. effort to moderate Soviet behavior, pressure is likely to mount for change in U.S. policy. There will be appeals from important segments of domestic opinion for a more "normal" U.S.-Soviet relationship, particularly in a period of political transition in Moscow.

It is therefore essential that the American people understand and support U.S. policy. This will require that official U.S. statements and actions avoid generating unrealizable expectations for near-term progress in the U.S.-Soviet relations. At the same time, the U.S. must demonstrate credibly that its policy is not a blueprint for an open-ended, sterile confrontation with Moscow, but a serious search for a stable and constructive long-term basis for U.S.-Soviet relations.

[Signed by Ronald Reagan]

1 ibid.

2 Fort Hood Shooter Nidal Hassan was an attendee of Dar al-Hijrah Mosque, and a student of Al Qaeda ideologue Anwar Al-Awlaki. Hazelton, L. (2009, November 9). Fort Hood gunman awake and talking as its revealed he 'attended same mosque in 2001 as September 11 hijackers' The Daily Mail. Retrieved January 13, 2015, from http://www.dailymail.co.uk/news/article-1225627/Fort-Hood-shootings-Army-major-Nidal-Malik-Hasan-kills-12-injures-31-shootout-troops-army-base.html

3 Dorell, O. (2013, April 25). Mosque that Boston suspects attended has radical ties. USA Today. Retrieved January 13, 2015, from http://www.usatoday.com/story/news/nation/2013/04/23/boston-mosque-radicals/2101411/

4 Geller, P. (2014, September 29). The Jihad Origins of the Oklahoma Beheaders Hamas Mosque. Breitbart. Retrieved January 13, 2015, from http://www.breitbart.com/national-security/2014/09/29/the-jihad-origins-of-the-oklahoma-beheaders-hamas-mosque/

5 The North American Islamic Trust was listed among "individuals/entities who are and/or were members of the US Muslim Brotherhood" on the "List of Unindicted Co-conspirators and/or Joint Venturers" as part of the Holy Land Foundation Trial. See: Trahan, J. (2010, November 26). Judge ruled prosecutors should not have publicly released Holy Land unindicted co-conspirators list. The Dallas Morning News. Retrieved January 13, 2015, from http://www.dallasnews.com/news/local-news/20101106-Judge-ruled-prosecutors-should-not-have-6808.ece

6 Eric Schmitt, "In Battle to Defang ISIS, U.S. Targets Its Psychology," New York Times, December 28, 2014.

7 Here in the United States, many Muslims have successfully assimilated. The Muslim Brotherhood has, therefore, sought to cultivate, or impose itself upon, a Muslim American population whose socio-economic status (household income, new business starts, consumption patterns, graduate degrees, and net worth) is consistently higher than the national average.

This community is made up of individuals who think of themselves mostly as Americans. But the Brotherhood wants them instead to see themselves as an oppressed and alienated minority. Countering this essential building block for the Brotherhood's civilization jihad by empowering truly assimilated Muslims and neutralizing the jihadis must be a high priority in the implementation of an NSDD 75 2.0.

8 As with any faith group, Muslims fall on a continuum of adherence to the commandments of their religion. Some, as within the Muslim Brotherhood network, project a fully shariah-compliant profile, whether that is deceptive or sincere being impossible to know. Others, especially in tolerant Western societies like the U.S. who also live in tolerant Islamic communities and families, are at liberty to consider themselves anything from marginally to completely secularized. Such individuals may limit their practice of Islam to its devotional and pietistic manifestations, perhaps including dietary regulations, but either in personal behavior or more or less openly expressed terms reject the supremacist aspects of shariah as well as the aggressive Dawah and jihad that it demands.

In terms of actual empirical data about such categorizations, however, the 2011 Pew Research Institute survey of Muslim Americans (http://www.people-press.org/2011/08/30/muslim-americans-no-signs-of-growth-in-alienation-or-support-for-extremism/) found that a startling 67% do *not* think of themselves as Americans first and Muslims second and 37% think there is only one way to interpret Islam. How exactly these numbers translate into shariah-compliant attitudes and behavior among Muslim Americans is a much harder question to answer without more specific data.

Wherever and however de facto repudiation of the supremacist Dawah-and-jihad elements of shariah may be recognized, and wherever possible fostered, however, it should be, as part of a strategy for fracturing and weakening the jihadis' ability to dominate and recruit from this community.

9 Egyptian President Al-Sisi at Al-Azhar: We Must Revolutionize Our Religion. (2014, December 28). Retrieved January 13, 2015, from http://www.memritv.org/clip_transcript/en/4704.htm

10 Shariah-Compliant Finance is used to generate obligatory tax payments (known as zakat) that provide underwriting for jihad. Moreover, by requiring equity partner ownership instead of interest-based loans in nations where a few families own all the shariah finance institutions, SCF effectively makes a small aristocracy the principal owners of all new ventures. This exacerbates a major source of the failure in economic development and lack of opportunity in such countries. When combined with overlapping shariah compliance boards among competing institutions – boards that have near-total visibility into bank and corporate operations – the result is often institutionalized corruption, conflicts of interest and serious security flaws. For more on problems associated with Shariah-Compliant Finance see, Yerushalmi, David, Shari'Ah's Black Box: Civil Liability and Criminal Exposure Surrounding Shari'Ah-Compliant Finance (March 2008). Utah Law Review, Forthcoming. Available at SSRN: http://ssrn.com/abstract=1105101

11 The five were Representatives Michele Bachmann (R-MN), Louie Gohmert(R-TX), Trent Franks (R-AZ), Lynn Westmoreland (R-GA) and Tom Rooney (R-FL). See: Gingrich, N. (2012, July 29). In defense of Michele Bachmann, Muslim Brotherhood probes. Politico. Retrieved January 13, 2015, from http://www.politico.com/news/stories/0712/79104.html

12 Yerushalmi, D., & Kedar, M. (2011). Shari'a and Violence in American Mosques. Middle East Quarterly, 18(3), 59-72.

13 The Naturalization Oath of Allegiance to the United States of America requires all naturalized citizens to swear, "that I will support and defend the Constitution and laws of the United States of America against all enemies, foreign and domestic; that I will bear true faith and allegiance to the same. . . ." See "TITLE 8 OF CODE OF FEDERAL REGULATIONS (8 CFR) \ 8 CFR PART 337 – OATH OF ALLEGIANCE \ § Sec. 337.1 Oath of allegiance, available at: http://www.uscis.gov/us-citizenship/naturalization-test/naturalization-oath-allegiance-united-states-america

14 Stalinsky, S. (2005, November 3). 'A World Without America'. Retrieved January 13, 2015, from http://jewishworldreview.com/1105/memri_world_san_america.php3

15 Sunni and Shiite Muslims, of course, differ on a number of points of theology. All four schools of Sunni Islam and the two schools of Shiite Islam, however, agree on the fundamentals of shariah, including the obligation to engage in or enable jihad. For more on the consensus among schools see: Resolution 152: Islam and the One Ummah and the Schools of Islamic Jurisprudence (Mathahib): (2004, November 9). The Amman Message. Retrieved January 13, 2015, from http://ammanmessage.com/index.php?option=com_content&task=view&id=35&Itemid=34

16 This dominating position of the centrality of shariah can best be seen in the "Cairo Declaration of Human Rights in Islam" adhered to by all 57 members of the Organization of Islamic Cooperation, which specifically excludes any permissible human rights outside the shariah. See: Cairo Declaration on Human Rights in Islam,Aug. 5, 1990, U.N. GAOR, World Conf. on Hum. Rts., 4th Sess., Agenda Item 5, U.N. Doc. A/CONF.157/PC/62/Add.18 (1993) available at: http://www1.umn.edu/humanrts/instree/cairodeclaration.html

17 National Security Directive 75. (1983, January 17). U.S. Relations with The USSR. Retrieved from http://www.reagan.utexas.edu/archives/reference/Scanned NSDDS/NSDD75.pdf

18 Sheetz, S. (2011, December 10). "We Win; They Lose": The Staggering Simplicity of Reagan's Grand Strategy. Retrieved January 13, 2015, from http://dailysignal.com/2011/12/10/we-win-they-lose-the-staggering-simplicity-of-reagan's-grand-strategy/

19 Pipes, Richard. "Team B: The Reality Behind the Myth." Commentary 82 (Oct. 1986): 25-40

20 "U.S. National Security Strategy," National Security Study Directive 1-82 (http://www.reagan.utexas.edu/archives/reference/Scanned%20NSSDs/NSSD1-82.pdf) and "U.S. Policy Toward the Soviet Union," National Security Study Directive 11-82 (http://www.reagan.utexas.edu/archives/reference/Scanned%20NSSDs/NSSD11-82.pdf).

21 "Response to NSSD 11-82: U.S. Relations with the USSR," National Security Council classified "Secret," December 6, 1982, pp. 1-43 (http://www.foia.cia.gov/sites/default/files/document_conversions/17/19821206.pdf).

22 National Security Directive 75. (1983, January 17). U.S. Relations with The USSR. Retrieved from http://www.reagan.utexas.edu/archives/reference/Scanned NSDDS/NSDD75.pdf

23 National Security Directive 75. (1983, January 17).

24 National Security Directive 75. (1983, January 17).

25 National Security Directive 75. (1983, January 17).

26 Other National Security Decision Directives concerning the Strategic Defense Initiative included NSDD 85, 116, 119 and 172. Each can be reviewed at: http://www.reagan.utexas.edu/archives/reference/NSDDs.html#.VKA2oOBAA, accessed on December 28, 2014.

27 Team B II. (2010). Shariah: The threat to America : An exercise in competitive analysis. Washington, DC: Center for Security Policy Press available at: http://shariahthethreat.org/wp-content/uploads/2011/04/Shariah-The-Threat-to-America-Team-B-Report-Web-09292010.pdf

28 Mura, Andrea (2012). "A genealogical inquiry into early Islamism: the discourse of Hasan al-Banna". Journal of Political Ideologies 17 (1): 61–85. doi:10.1080/13569317.2012.644986.

29 Qutb, S. (2006). Milestones (Special Edition) (A. Mehri, Ed.). Birmingham: Maktabah Booksellers. Available at: http://www.kalamullah.com/Books/Milestones%20Special%20Edition.pdf

30 Azzam, A. (2002). Defence of the Muslim lands (2nd English ed.). London: Azzam Publications available at: http://www.religioscope.com/info/doc/jihad/azzam_defence_2_intro.htm

31 Malik, S. (1979). The Quranic concept of war. Lahore: Wajidalis available at: https://www.yumpu.com/pt/document/view/7647367/malik-quranic-concept-of-war.

32 For more analysis on The Quranic Concept of War See: Myers, J. (2006). The Quranic Concept of War. Parameters, Winter (2006-2007), 108-127. Retrieved January 13, 2015, from http://strategicstudiesinstitute.army.mil/pubs/parameters/Articles/06winter/win-ess.pdf

33 "UAE Publishes List of Terrorist Organizations," Gulf News, 15 November 2014, URL: http://gulfnews.com/news/gulf/uae/government/uae-publishes-list-of-terrorist-organisations-1.1412895, accessed 15 November 2014.

34 Zvi Mazel, "Analysis: When the West and Arab Nations Differ," Jerusalem Post, November 24, 2014.

35 The complete listing of evidentiary documents is available at: "Judges Notable Cases: USA V. Holy Land Foundation" United States District Court Court of North Texas. accessed at: http://www.txnd.uscourts.gov/judges/hlf2.html

36 See www.MuslimBrotherhoodinAmerica.com Part 8.

37 Our Team page of Freedom and Justice Foundation, Plano, Texas webpage, 22 June 2007, URL: https://web.archive.org/web/20081211064713/http://www.freeandjust.org/OurTeam.htm, accessed 26 September 2011. Note: President, CEO and Co-founder.

38 Mohamed Elibiary, "What Would You Say to America's Leading Islamophobes if Given the Opportunity," Muslim Matters, 6 February 2008, URL: http://muslimmatters.org/2008/02/06/what-would-you-say-to-america's-leading-islamophobes-if-given-the-opportunity/, accessed 27 June 2014. States in "About Mohamed Elibiary":

Mohamed Elibiary co-founded the Freedom and Justice Foundation (F&J) in November 2002 to promote a Centrist Public Policy environment in Texas by coordinating the state level government and interfaith community relations for the organized Texas Muslim community. In 2005, Mohamed spearheaded the launching of the Texas Islamic Council (T.I.C.) as an F&J program for Muslim congregations, which has quickly grown to become the state's largest Muslim network encompassing 100,000 Texans. As Coordinator of the T.I.C., Mohamed developed working relationships with similar faith-based entities around Texas including the Texas Conference of Churches, Texas Catholic Conference and the Baptist General Convention of Texas.

In 2006, the 16 largest Muslim congregations and civic organizations in the Dallas-Fort Worth area followed this example by creating a collective representative body called the North Texas Islamic Council (NTIC) and Mohamed was elected to its 7 member executive governing body. Since 2005, Mohamed, as a National Security Policy Analyst, has been advising intelligence and law enforcement agencies (ex. FBI, DHS, NCTC, ODNI, etc.) on various Counterterrorism (CT) issues (ex. Domestic Intelligence, Strategic Intelligence Analysis, Information Sharing and Radicalization).

39 Screen Capture, CAIR DFW webpage dated 12 April 2003, in article by Ryan Mauro, "Senior Homeland Security Advisor Formerly CAIR Official," The Clarion Project, 1 December 2013, URL: http://www.clarionproject.org/analysis/senior-homeland-security-adviser-formerly-cair-official, accessed 19 August 2014. Note: screen capture identifies Elibiary as Committee Chairman.

40 Form 990 Documenting Mohamed Elibiary's Status as Board Member on CAIR Dallas-Fort Worth Chapter –FY 2003, IRS Form 990 (2003) copy at The Clarion Project Archives, URL: http://www.clarionproject.org/document/990-form-proving-mohamed-Elibiary-worked-cair, accessed 19 August 2014. Note: Identifies Elibiary as Board Member.

41 Letter to John Brennan, Assistant to the President for Homeland Security and Counterterrorism and Deputy National Security Advisor, The White House, signed by, among others, numerous organizations known to be associated with the Muslim Brotherhood, PDF document dated 19 October 2011: "We urge you to create an interagency taskforce, led by the White House, tasked with the following responsibilities: 2. Purge all federal government training materials of biased materials; 3. Implement a mandatory re-training program for FBI agents, U.S. Army officers, and all federal, state and local law enforcement who have been subjected to biased training; 4. Ensure that personnel reviews are conducted and all trainers and other government employees who promoted biased trainers and training materials are effectively disciplined; 5. Implement quality control processes to ensure that bigoted trainers and biased materials are not developed or utilized in the future; ..."

42 Letter to Farhana Khera from John Brennan, the White House, 3 November 2011.

43 Letter to Farhana Khera from John Brennan, the White House, 3 November 2011.

44 ISNA & Nat. Orgs. Meet With FBI Dir. To Discuss Biased FBI Training Materials," ISNA Press Release, ISNA, 14 February 2012, Url: http://counterjihadreport.com/2012/02/14/isna-nat-orgs-meet-with-fbi-dir-to-discuss-biased-fbi-training-materials/.

45 71-022, 112th Congress, Report House of Representatives, 1st Session, 112-284: Agriculture, Rural Development, Food and Drug Administration, and Related Agencies Programs for the Fiscal Year Ending September 30, 2012, and for Other

Purposes, 14 November 2011- Ordered to be printed, to accompany H.R. 2112, signed 18 November 2011, URL: http://thomas.loc.gov/cgi-bin/cpquery/T?&report=hr284&dbname =112& states: "Liaison partnerships - The conferees support the FBI's policy prohibiting any formal non-investigative cooperation with unindicted co-conspirators in terrorism cases. The conferees expect the FBI to insist on full compliance with this policy by FBI field offices and to report to the Committees on Appropriations regarding any violation of the policy."

46 FBI Director Mueller, Testimony, "House Judiciary Committee Holds Hearing on Oversight of the FBI," Congressional Hearings, CQ Congressional Transcripts, 9 May 2012. Read: Mueller "So it is not as if we have purged a substantial amount of our training materials."

47 David Alexander, "Military Instructor Suspended over Islam Course," Reuters, 20 June 2012, http://www.reuters.com/article/2012/06/20/us-usa-defense-islam-idUSBRE85J0XJ20120620, accessed 20 June 2012.

48 http://www.muslimadvocates.org/files/FINALCoalitionLetterTrainings_8.14.14.pdf

49 Mohamed Elibiary, Mohamed Elibiary Tweet, @MohamedElibiary Twitter, 16 November 2014, URL: https://twitter.com/MohamedElibiary/status/533768748159995904, accessed 16 November 2014. States: "#PT As was published in media interviews, I've sat thru USG briefings on MB in US & did my own field research. US won't follow UAE bullshit."

50 Mohamed Elibiary, Mohamed Elibiary Tweet, @MohamedElibiary Twitter, 16 November 2014, URL: https://twitter.com/MohamedElibiary/status/533768748159995904, accessed 16 November 2014. States: "#PT As was published in media interviews, I've sat thru USG briefings on MB in US & did my own field research. US won't follow UAE bullshit."

51 Kredo, Adam, "Controversial DHS Advisor Let Go Amid Allegations of Cover Up," The Washington Free Beacon, September 15, 2014, URL: http://freebeacon.com/issues/controversial-dhs-adviser-let-go-amid-allegations-of-cover-up/

52 Paragraph 3, Section VII, "Combating Islamophobia," The Third Extraordinary Session of the Islamic Summit, Makka Almukarama, Organization of the Islamic Conference, 7-8 December 2005, URL: http://www.oic-oci.org/ex-summit/english/10-years-plan.htm. Cited hereafter as Third Extraordinary Session, "Section VII, Combating Islamophobia." Reads: Endeavor to have the United Nations adopt an international resolution to counter Islamophobia and to call upon all states to enact laws to counter it, including deterrent punishment.

53 Secretary of State Hillary Clinton, "Remarks at the Organization of the Islamic Conference (OIC) High-Level Meeting on Combating Religious Intolerance," Given at the Center for Islamic Arts and History, Istanbul, Turkey, United States Department of State Release, 15 July 2011, http://www.state.gov/secretary/rm/2011/07/168636.htm, accessed July 21 2011.

54 Secretary of State Hillary Clinton, "Remarks at the Organization of the Islamic Conference (OIC) High-Level Meeting on Combating Religious Intolerance," Given at the Center for Islamic Arts and History, Istanbul, Turkey, United States Department of State Release, 15 July 2011, http://www.state.gov/secretary/rm/2011/07/168636.htm, accessed July 21 2011.

55 "High Ranking DOJ Official Refuses to Affirm 1st Amendment Rights," Representative Trent Franks, YouTube published by Rep Trent Franks, 26 July 2012, http://www.youtube.com/watch?v=0wwv9I6W8yc&feature=player_embedded, accessed 27 July 2012.

56 "Remarks by the President to the UN General Assembly," given at the United Nations Headquarters, New York, New York, For Immediate Release, Office of the Press Secretary, The White House, 25 September 2012, URL: http://www.whitehouse.gov/the-press-office/2012/09/25/remarks-president-un-general-assembly, accessed 4 October 2012.

57 Feferberg, E. (2013, January 22). Everyone Will Fight, African Troops, U.S. Airlift Join Mali Operation. New York Times. Retrieved January 13, 2015, from http://worldnews.nbcnews.com/_news/2013/01/22/16646479-everyone-will-fight-african-troops-us-airlift-join-mali-operation?lite

58 Associated Press. (2014, May 21). Boko Haram kills 48, U.S. Expands Drone Search for abducted Girls. CBC News. Retrieved January 13, 2015, from http://www.cbc.ca/news/world/boko-haram-kills-48-u-s-expands-drone-search-for-abducted-girls-1.2649136

59 Scott Tyson, A. (2005, July 26). U.S. Pushes Anti-Terrorism in Africa. The Washington Post. Retrieved January 13, 2015, from http://www.washingtonpost.com/wp-dyn/content/article/2005/07/25/AR2005072501801.html

60 Letsch, C., James, C., Lewis, P., & Watt, N. (2014, October 6). Syrian Kurds say air strikes against ISIS are not working. The Guardian. Retrieved January 13, 2015, from http://www.theguardian.com/world/2014/oct/05/air-strikes-isis-not-working-syrian-kurds, and Boyle, D. (2014, October 1). US cannot tell how effective airstrikes against ISIS have been because of huge gaps in intelligence, officials claim. The Daily Mail. Retrieved January 13, 2015, from

http://www.dailymail.co.uk/news/article-2776282/US-tell-effective-airstrikes-against-ISIS-huge-gaps-intelligence-officials-claim.html

61 Simoes, H. (2014, May 16). Why the military can't get enough of Amphibious Ready Groups. Stars and Stripes. Retrieved January 13, 2015, from http://www.stripes.com/news/why-the-military-can-t-get-enough-of-amphibious-ready-groups-1.283110

62 United States Congress. House of Representatives. Armed Services Committee (2014): Majority Interim Report: Benghazi Investigation Update: Findings. February 2014. Washington D.C.: Government Printing Office, Pg. 2.

63 Starr, B. (2013, April 25). U.S. Marine Rapid Response Force Deploying to Spain Base. Retrieved January 13, 2015, from http://security.blogs.cnn.com/2013/04/25/u-s-marine-rapid-response-force-deploying-to-spain-base/

64 Wong, K. (2013, January 1). Navy to stretch deployments; aircraft carrier fleet down to 9. The Washington Times. Retrieved January 13, 2015, from http://www.washingtontimes.com/news/2013/jan/10/navy-stretch-deployments/?page=all

65 For example, the Training and Doctrine Command (TRADOC) employed a well-known Muslim Brotherhood operative, Louay Safi, as an instructor for thousands of Army officers and senior NCOs, to train them in the "proper" understanding of Islam prior to their deployments to Iraq and Afghanistan. The instructor who blew the whistle on Safi was terminated from the training program. By contrast, TRADOC properly employed Pashtun instructors to instruct officers and NCOs in how to use the Pashtunwali cultural code for military purposes in Afghanistan. For more on Louay Safi see, Poole, P. (2010, November 1). 10 Failures of the U.S. Government on the Domestic Islamist Threat. Retrieved January 13, 2015, from http://www.centerforsecuritypolicy.org/upload/wysiwyg/article pdfs/10_Failures_Patrick_Poole_1115.pdf

66 Al-Jabouri, N., & Jensen, S. (2004). The Iraqi and AQI Roles in the Sunni Awakening.PRISM, 3(18), 9-9. Retrieved January 13, 2015, from http://cco.dodlive.mil/files/2014/02/Prism_3-18_Al-Jabouri_Jensen.pdf

67 Schmitt, E. (2004, April 20). U.S. Commanders Say Increased Border Patrols Are Halting the Influx of Non-Iraqi Guerrillas. The New York Times. Retrieved January 13, 2015, from http://www.nytimes.com/2004/04/20/world/struggle-for-iraq-infiltration-us-commanders-say-increased-border-patrols-are.html

68 The Washington Times. (2014, June 24). 'Taliban' rule imposed on Fallujah. Washington Times. Retrieved January 13, 2015, from http://www.washingtontimes.com/news/2004/jun/24/20040624-112923-9113r/?page=all

69 MacAskill, E. (2003, April 25). US accuses Iran of stirring up protests. The Guardian. Retrieved January 13, 2015, from http://www.theguardian.com/world/2003/apr/25/iraq.iran

70 United States Commission on International Religious Freedom. (2006, March 1). Iraq's Permanent Constitution: Analysis and Recommendations. Retrieved January 13, 2015, from http://www.uscirf.gov/reports-briefs/special-reports/iraqs-permanent-constitution-march-2006 On the role in U.S. advisors on producing the document see: Brand, M. (2005, August 23). Next Step for Iraq's Constitution Writers. National Public Radio. Retrieved January 13, 2015, from http://www.npr.org/templates/story/story.php?storyId=4811914

71 Perry, W., & Abizaid, J. co-chairmen (2014, July 31). Ensuring a Strong National Defense. : The National Defense Panel Review of the 2014 Quadrennial Defense Review. Retrieved January 13, 2015, from http://www.usip.org/sites/default/files/Ensuring-a-Strong-U.S.-Defense-for-the-Future-NDP-Review-of-the-QDR_0.pdf

72 Ibid.

73 Gertz, B. (2014, March 13). F-35 Secrets Now Showing Up in China's Stealth Fighter. The Washington Times. Retrieved January 13, 2015, from http://www.washingtontimes.com/news/2014/mar/13/f-35-secrets-now-showing-chinas-stealth-fighter/?page=all

74 U.S. Naval Institute. (2009, March 31). Report: Chinese Develop Special "Kill Weapon" to Destroy U.S. Aircraft Carriers. Retrieved January 13, 2015, from http://www.usni.org/news-and-features/chinese-kill-weapon

75 Secretary of Defense Hagel, C. (2014, November 15). Reagan National Defense Forum Keynote. Retrieved January 13, 2015, from http://www.defense.gov/Speeches/Speech.aspx?SpeechID=1903

76 New Deterrent Working Group. (2009). U.S. Nuclear Deterrence in the 21st Century Getting it Right (pp. 23-26). Washington: Center for Security Policy Press.

77 Winter, M. (2014, December 2). Report: Iran Hacking Key U.S. , Global Firms. USA Today. Retrieved January 13, 2015, from http://www.usatoday.com/story/news/world/2014/12/02/iran-hackers-infiltrate-energy-transport-infrastructure/19806247/

78 Gaffney, F. (2014). A Congressional Look Back at 2014, With Rep. Trent Franks [Radio series episode]. In Secure Freedom Radio. Washington, from http://www.centerforsecuritypolicy.org/2014/12/22/a-congressional-look-back-at-2014-with-rep-trent-franks/

79 Phillips, T. (2014, July 23). Near Miss: The Solar Superstorm of July 2012. Retrieved January 13, 2015, from http://science.nasa.gov/science-news/science-at-nasa/2014/23jul_superstorm/

80 Office of the Press Secretary. (2014, September 10). Statement by the President of the United States on ISIL. Retrieved January 13, 2015, from http://www.whitehouse.gov/the-press-office/2014/09/10/statement-president-isil-1

81 Gertz, B. (2014, October 7). Surrender in the War of Ideas. The Washington Free Beacon. Retrieved January 13, 2015, from http://freebeacon.com/national-security/surrender-in-the-war-of-ideas/

82 ibid.

83 Sargant, W. (1997). Battle for the mind: A physiology of conversion and brain-washing. Cambridge, MA: Malor Books.

84 Harry S. Truman Papers Staff Member and Office Files: Psychological Strategy Board Files. "Presidential Directive Dated April 4, 1941," Retrieved January 13, 2015, from http://www.trumanlibrary.org/hstpaper/physc.htm

85 Schoen, F., & Lamb, C. (2012). Deception, Disinformation, and Strategic Communications: How One Interagency Group Made a Major Difference. Strategic Perspectives, 11. Retrieved January 13, 2015, from http://ndupress.ndu.edu/Portals/68/Documents/stratperspective/inss/Strategic-Perspectives-11.pdf

86 Halper, S. (2013, May 1). China: The Three Warfares. The Office of Net Assessment. Retrieved January 13, 2015, from http://images.smh.com.au/file/2014/04/11/5343124/China_%20The%20three%20warfares.pdf?rand=1397212645609

87 See for example: Pomerantsev, P. (2015, January 1). Inside Putin's Information War. The Politico. Retrieved January 13, 2015, from http://www.politico.com/magazine/story/2015/01/putin-russia-tv-113960_Page3.html#ixzz3NwoujHo0

88 Cull, N. (2012). The Decline and Fall of the United States Information Agency: American Public Diplomacy 1989-2001. Palgrave-MacMillian.

89 Kredo, A. (2014, October 17). Congress Calls for Investigation into VOA for Pro-Iran Corruption. The Washington Free Beacon. Retrieved January 13, 2015, from http://freebeacon.com/national-security/congress-calls-for-investigation-into-voa-for-pro-iran-corruption/

90 Scarborough, R. (2013, April 25). Obama's Scrub of Muslim Terms under question; common links in attacks. The Washington Times. Retrieved January 13, 2015, from http://www.washingtontimes.com/news/2013/apr/25/obamas-cleansing-of-islamic-terms-suppresses-commo/?page=all

91 Wolf, Z. (2011, February 10). Director of National Intelligence James Clapper: Muslim Brotherhood "Largely Secular". ABC News. Retrieved January 13, 2015, from http://abcnews.go.com/blogs/politics/2011/02/director-of-national-intelligence-james-clapper-muslim-brotherhood-largely-secular/

92 DOD Independent Review. (2010, January 10). Protecting The Force: Lessons from Fort Hood. Retrieved January 13, 2015, from http://www.defense.gov/pubs/pdfs/DOD-ProtectingTheForce-Web_Security_HR_13Jan10.pdf

93 Picket, K. (2012, September 24). Muslim Advocacy Groups Influence Heavily on U.S. National Security Protocol and Lexicon. The Washington Times. Retrieved January 13, 2015, from http://www.washingtontimes.com/blog/watercooler/2012/sep/24/picket-muslim-advocacy-groups-influence-heavily-us/

94 Judicial Watch. (2014, April 29). Judicial Watch: Benghazi Documents Point to White House on Misleading Talking Points. Retrieved January 13, 2015, from http://www.judicialwatch.org/press-room/press-releases/judicial-watch-benghazi-documents-point-white-house-misleading-talking-points/

95 Taylor, G. (2014, March 31). CIA officer confirmed no protests before misleading Benghazi account given. The Washington Times. Retrieved January 13, 2015, from http://www.washingtontimes.com/news/2014/mar/31/cia-ignored-station-chief-in-libya-when-creating-t/

96 The Editors. (2004, September 29). Editorial: The CIA's Insurgency. The Washington Times. Retrieved January 13, 2015, from http://www.wsj.com/articles/SB109641497779730745

97 Gertz, B. (2002). Breakdown: How America's intelligence failures led to September 11. Washington, D.C.: Regnery Pub.

98 Gertz, B. (2007, March 9). Inside the Ring: Sutter criticized. The Washington Times. Retrieved January 13, 2015, from http://www.gertzfile.com/gertzfile/ring030907.html

99 Fixing the damage done by this statute, though necessary, is likely to prove to be a time-consuming and, therefore, longer-term project. Consequently, the assumption of this paper is that implementation of the new counter-ideology strategy will have

to be accomplished within, and despite, the current intelligence community structure.

100 Musharbash, Y. (2005, August 12). The Future of Terrorism: What Al-Qaida Really Wants. Der Spiegel. Retrieved January 13, 2015, from http://www.spiegel.de/international/the-future-of-terrorism-what-al-qaida-really-wants-a-369448.html

101 Musharbash, Y.

102 'Claim jobseeker's allowance and plan holy war': Hate preacher pocketing £25,000 a year in benefits calls on fanatics to live off the state. (2013, February 17). The Daily Mail. Retrieved January 13, 2015, from http://www.dailymail.co.uk/news/article-2279972/Anjem-Choudary-Hate-preacher-pocketing-25-000-year-benefits-calls-fanatics-live-state.html

103 Dilanian, K. (2014, September 14). Islamic State's Funding Exceeds That Of Any Other Terrorist Group In History. The Huffington Post. Retrieved January 13, 2015, from http://www.huffingtonpost.com/2014/09/14/islamic-state-funding_n_5818462.html

104 Shariah Compliant Finance | Shariah: The Threat to America. (n.d.). Retrieved January 13, 2015, from http://shariahthethreat.org/shariah-compliant-finance/

105 Musharbash, Y. (2013, March 20). Bisher unbekanntes Al-Kaida-Dokument enthüllt Strategie für globale Anschläge. Zeit Online. Retrieved January 13, 2015, from http://www.zeit.de/politik/ausland/2013-03/terror-al-kaida-anschlagsplaene

106 Gertz, B. (2014, October 28). Al Qaeda Targets Oil Tankers, Sea Lanes. Retrieved January 13, 2015, from http://freebeacon.com/national-security/al-qaeda-targets-oil-tankers-sea-lanes/

107 Al-Naimi: OPEC 'must combat US shale boom'. (2014, November 29). Arab News. Retrieved January 13, 2015, from http://www.arabnews.com/news/667156

108 Madhani, A. (2014, October 14). Shariah financing growing popular in the West. USA Today. Retrieved January 13, 2015, from http://www.usatoday.com/story/money/business/2014/10/11/shariah-compliant-islamic-financing-usa-europe/16828599/

109 See, for example: Gewertz, K. (2002, May 2). Seminar explores Islamic finance: Westerners learn basics about growing practice. Harvard Gazette. Retrieved January 13, 2015, from http://news.harvard.edu/gazette/2002/05.02/12-islamic.html

110 ISIS unveils gold-backed currency to break off from Western economies that 'enslaved Muslims' (2014, November 14). NY Daily News. Retrieved January 13,

2015, from http://www.nydailynews.com/news/world/isis-unveils-gold-backed-currency-article-1.2010929

111 UAE Designates CAIR, MAS as Terrorist Groups. (2014, November 17). Retrieved January 13, 2015, from http://www.investigativeproject.org/4655/uae-designates-cair-mas-as-terrorist-groups

112 Boghardt, L. (2014, May 2). The Terrorist Funding Disconnect with Qatar and Kuwait. Retrieved January 13, 2015, from http://www.washingtoninstitute.org/policy-analysis/view/the-terrorist-funding-disconnect-with-qatar-and-kuwait

113 Nashat, S. (n.d.). Structured Islamic Finance. The Counsel Magazine.

114 For an excellent treatment of this point, see Bruce Thornton, "Why We Should Study War," The Hoover Institution, November 2013 Available at: http://www.hoover.org/research/why-should-we-study-war

115 Diana West, American Betrayal: The Secret Assault on Our Nation's Character, St. Martin's Press 2014.

116 Herridge, C. (2014, December 19). Evidence in Sony hack attack suggests possible involvement by Iran, China or Russia, intel source says. Retrieved January 13, 2015, from http://www.foxnews.com/politics/2014/12/19/fbi-points-digital-finger-at-north-korea-for-sony-hacking-attack-formal/

117 Boyer, Dave, "White House threatens 'proportional' response to North Korea cyberattacks on Sony Pictures," Washington Times, December 18, 2014. Retrieved January 6, 2015 from http://www.washingtontimes.com/news/2014/dec/18/white-house-threatens-proportional-response-north-/?page=all

118 Presidential Policy Directive/PPD-8: National Preparedness, March 30, 2011. Retrieved January 6 2015 from http://www.dhs.gov/presidential-policy-directive-8-national-preparedness

119 National Strategy for Counterterrorism, June 2011 retrieved January 6 2015 from http://www.whitehouse.gov/sites/default/files/counterterrorism_strategy.pdf accessed 6 January 2015.

120 Authorization for the Use of Military Force, September 18, 2001. Retrieved January 6, 2015 from http://www.gpo.gov/fdsys/pkg/PLAW-107publ40/pdf/PLAW-107publ40.pdf

121 United States Department of Defense. (2013, April 15). Retrieved January 13, 2015, from http://www.defense.gov/news/newsarticle.aspx?id=119776

122 Elgin, Ben and Michael Riley, "Now at the Sands Casino: An Iranian Hacker in Every Server," 11 December 2014. URL at http://www.businessweek.com/articles/2014-12-11/iranian-hackers-hit-sheldon-adelsons-sands-casino-in-las-vegas accessed 22 December 2014.

123 Operation Cleaver, Cylance. URL at http://www.cylance.com/operation-cleaver/ accessed 22 December 2014.

124 Gore, Leada, "FBI warns defense firms of 'coordinated' cyber attacks traced to Iran," December 18, 2014. URL at http://www.al.com/news/index.ssf/2014/12/fbi_warns_defense_firms_of_coo.html accessed 22 December 2014.

125 "Update on Sony Investigation," FBI, December 19, 2014. URL at http://www.fbi.gov/news/pressrel/press-releases/update-on-sony-investigation accessed 22 December 2014.

126 Perlroth, Nicole and David Sanger, "Attack is Suspected as North Korean Internet Collapses," Dec. 22, 2014. URL at http://www.nytimes.com/2014/12/23/world/asia/attack-is-suspected-as-north-korean-internet-collapses.html?_r=1 accessed 22 December 2014.

127 Cyber Chair Meehan: Sony Hack Shows "Dire Need" to Upgrade Cybersecurity Defenses. (2014, December 18). Retrieved January 13, 2015, from http://meehan.house.gov/media-center/press-releases/cyber-chair-meehan-sony-hack-shows-dire-need-to-upgrade-cybersecurity

128 "Hack attack causes 'massive damage' at steel works," BBC, 22 December 2014. URL at http://www.bbc.com/news/technology-30575104 accessed 22 December 2014.

129 Henn, S. (2014, December 26). Sony Hack Highlights The Global Underground Market For Malware. Retrieved January 13, 2015, from http://www.npr.org/blogs/alltechconsidered/2014/12/26/373073150/sony-hack-highlights-the-global-underground-market-for-malware

130 Woolsey, Ambassador R. James, "From Al Qaeda to the Islamic State, Jihadi Groups Engage In Cyber Jihad: An Introduction," written as lead-in to the December 2014 report, "From Al-Qaeda To The Islamic State (ISIS), Jihadi Groups Engage in Cyber Jihad: Beginning With 1980s Promotion of Use of 'Electronic Technologies' Up to Today's Embrace of Social Media to Attract a New Jihadi Generation," by Steven Stalinsky and R. Sosnow for MEMRI (Middle East Media Research Institute). Retrieved December 22, 2014 from http://cjlab.memri.org/analysis-and-special-reports/cyber-jihad/

131 See the 4th issue of the Islamic State's Web magazine Dabiq for an explanation of this End Times eschatology. Retrieved December 22, 2014 from https://ia601403.us.archive.org/0/items/Dabiq04En/Dabiq_04_en.pdf

132 See here the website of the Industrial Areas Foundation, which Alinsky founded in 1940: http://www.industrialareasfoundation.org/

133 The world from here: Hamas and BDS. (2014, March 4). Retrieved January 13, 2015, from http://www.jpost.com/Opinion/Columnists/The-world-from-here-Hamas-and-BDS-344303

134 Sharkov, Damien, "ISIS Urge Ferguson Rioters to 'Be Like Malcom X,'" Newsweek, 11/26/14. Retrieved December 22, 2015 from http://www.newsweek.com/isis-urge-ferguson-rioters-be-malcolm-x-287257

135 In a youtube video of World Workers Party Organizer Larry Holmes, Holmes discusses the party's role in organizing for Ferguson. WWPVideo. (2014, November 21). Stand With Ferguson. Retrieved January 13, 2015, from http://youtu.be/BXClUboG97Y For more background on the World Worker's Party see: Stephen Schwartz, "Who Pays for these demonstrations" Frontpage Magazine, January 24, 2003, Retrieved January 13, 2015 from http://archive.frontpagemag.com/readArticle.aspx?ARTID=20117

136 US Muslim Brotherhood Political Party Convenes for Inaugural Banquet in Washington, DC Area," Center for Security Policy, June 30, 2014. URL at http://www.centerforsecuritypolicy.org/2014/06/30/u-s-muslim-brotherhood-political-party-convenes-for-inaugural-banquet-in-washington-dc-area/ accessed 22 December 2014.

137 "US Muslim Brotherhood Political Party Protests in Chicago against Israel and Jews," Center for Security Policy, July 28, 2014. URL at http://www.centerforsecuritypolicy.org/2014/07/28/us-muslim-brotherhood-political-party-protests-in-chicago-against-israel-and-jews/ accessed 22 December 2014.

138 Shanker, Thom, "Cyberwar Nominee Sees Gap in Law," New York Times, April 14, 2010. Retrieved January 6, 2014, from http://www.nytimes.com/2010/04/15/world/15military.html

139 Brennan, LTC John W., "United States Counter Terrorism Cyber Law and Policy, Enabling or Disabling?" US Army War College, 15 March 2012. Retrieved Janaury 6, 2015 from http://nsfp.web.unc.edu/files/2012/09/Brennan_UNITED-STATES-COUNTER-TERRORISM-CYBER-LAW-AND-POLICY.pdf

140 Akram, M. (1991). An explanatory memorandum on the general strategic goal for the group in North America. This document originally dated May 22nd, 1991 was

introduced into evidence as "Elbarasse Search #3" by federal prosecutors in the Holy Land Foundation trial in Dallas in 2008. Available at: http://www.txnd.uscourts.gov/judges/hlf2/09-25-08/Elbarasse%20Search%203.pdf

140 ibid.

141 M. Fethullah Gulen, Prophet Muhammad as COMMANDER, Kaynak (Izmir), Turkey, 1998.

142 Shariah in American Courts: The Expanding Influence of Islamic Law in U.S. Jurisprudence, Center for Security Policy Press, 2014.

143 See Muslim Brotherhood in America, www.MuslimBrotherhoodinAmerica.com, and Agent of Influence: Grover Norquist and The Assault on the Right, Center for Security Policy Press, 2014.

144 Franks Statement on IG Letters Concerning Muslim Brotherhood. (2012, July 20). Retrieved January 13, 2015, from https://franks.house.gov/press-release/franks-statement-ig-letters-concerning-muslim-brotherhood

145 See, for example, Miller, S. (2012, July 18). McCain Defends Clinton Aide Huma Abedin Against Bachmann Accusation About Muslim Brotherhood. Retrieved January 14, 2015, from http://abcnews.go.com/blogs/politics/2012/07/mccain-defends-clinton-aide-huma-abedin-against-house-gop-charges-of-muslim-brotherhood-scheme/

146 "Muslim Brotherhood Terrorist Designation Act of 2014" July 24, 2014, Retrieved January 14, 2015, from http://freebeacon.com/wp-content/uploads/2014/07/2014-July-24-MB-FTO-FINAL.pdf

147 Yerushalmi, D., & Kedar, M. (2011). Shari'a and Violence in American Mosques. Middle East Quarterly, 18(3), 59-72.

Made in the USA
Middletown, DE
04 April 2015